The Dance at Mociu

ALSO BY PETER RILEY

POETRY
Love-Strife Machine
The Canterbury Experimental Weekend
The Linear Journal
The Musicians, The Instruments
Preparations
Lines on the Liver
Tracks and Mineshafts
Ospita
Noon Province
Sea Watches
Reader
Lecture
Sea Watch Elegies
Royal Signals
Distant Points
Alstonefield
Between Harbours
Noon Province et autres poèmes
Snow Has Settled ... Bury Me Here
Author
Passing Measures: A Collection of Poems
The Sea's Continual Code
Aria with Small Lights
Alstonefield (extended edition)
Excavations
A Map of Faring
The Llyn Writings
The Day's Final Balance: Uncollected Writings 1965-2006
Best at Night Alone
Western States
Twelve Moons
Greek Passages
The Derbyshire Poems
The Glacial Stairway

PROSE
Two Essays
Company Week

Peter Riley

The Dance at Mociu

Shearsman Books

Published in the United Kingdom in 2014 by
Shearsman Books
50 Westons Hill Drive
Emersons Green
BRISTOL
BS16 7DF

www.shearsman.com

Second Edition.
First edition published in 2003,
in association with Gratton Street Irregulars.

ISBN 978-1-84861-386-7

ACKNOWLEDGEMENTS
Some of these pieces have appeared in
Junction Box (online), *Oasis, Notre Dame Review* and *PN Review.*

for Beryl

Introduction

One response you may have to this collection of factual encounters with the people and ways of Transylvania, might be to travel to the place yourself. However this would be to misunderstand the peculiar responsibility of the writer. Your experience could turn out to be entirely different to that depicted here; the place would literally not be the same for you, and this book misleading. Peter Riley's perceptions of the wooden villages and peasants of the region are distinctive to his relationship with them. Suffice to say this is not a travel book, he is not a guide and you may need this book in your life for quite other reasons.

When the separate accounts first appeared as pamphlets and in personal letters, I found something in them that I wanted; firstly the importance of music in the community and then, as the pieces grew, a non-dramatic and literal depiction of the meaning of wealth and poverty. Behind both discoveries is the core of the book, a community living as one rather than as random individuals.

The music of Maramureş is alive and embedded in the shared lives of the villagers. It is, suggestively, an element in lives which are not lived separately, and draws the common experience into a different significance. Music is there at funerals, weddings and any other events, and along with alcohol is the medium of festive time — the occasion that stands against linear experience but draws the day to day into itself. Significant events are marked in festive time; all weddings become one wedding, all deaths one death.

That music can have such meaning is not commonplace in the west. In Maramureş for instance, as in other parts of the Balkans through to the southern Greek mainland, the dead of marriageable age are married to death, they become death's spouse and wedding songs accompany the funeral. The custom is glimpsed in 'The Funeral'. No claims as anthropologist are made, but the significance is unavoidable. "I get a feeling that funerals are common, that everybody knows exactly what to do and what comes next." Funerals are not the only occasions depicted for such certainty of behaviour; it is a characteristic feature of the community.

The view of the autochthonic music setting arising here is quite different from the currently popular commodification of the world-music scene, which elects only one Romanian gypsy band, only one kora player and only one narwhal blow hole soloist, and only if the artist/celebrity is photogenic. The scene here is plural, hybrid, organised and unpredictable but with everybody seeming to know what to do. Typically *Event at Deseşti,* within which music plays its usual, striking part, owes more to affectionate comedy than classical anthropology.

The other element here which first struck me, is the encounter with the cataclysmic tilting of wealth to the west and what it does to the poor from elsewhere. That there is a new sub-class of the dispossessed working in various forms of legal and illegal poverty in the West is well known. That the internationalised poor are drawn from communities in part impoverished by globalisation is also obvious. In the Maramureş of old Europe Peter Riley sees for himself the lives caught up in the issue. To glamorise poverty is a rich person's idiotic indulgence; to see the wealth of the west as the only richness is a different sort of mistake shared by the rich and poor.

Alongside this dilemma about what the young are to do is the overwhelming generosity of the peasants towards their visitors. Strangers are here to be looked after, "…in this small zone of wooden villages operating a system of land tenure considered about a thousand years out of date where we come from…" In comparison we are poor because we are ungenerous and distrustful. "We have lost it, and we live alone…" puts its finger on the essential difference between our present conditions. In fact the contrast is even more abject in 'These People', where again courtesy and generosity towards the stranger is exemplified but if these people should look for well-paid work in Britain they know they are treated as "vermin." We should be ashamed of our government and those individuals and institutions holding such attitudes. In these detailed, intimate and personal encounters is a whole world of quite other value, dependent upon the "possibility of remaining self-sufficient, of just about managing, with very little help from the town, and that at a high rate, but in circles of light."

Kelvin Corcoran

Contents

Preface

Most of them I call "factual stories". That is to say, things did happen more-or-less as described (or failed to, or appeared to, both of which I accept), and personal and place names are unaltered, but they remain constructed things. Those I don't call factual stories I call prose-poems, which means that nothing at all happened but there was a certain something in the air. We went there in search of music; everything else was glimpsed out of the corner of the eye, and hung on the frailty of singular instances. But instances which clearly could not occur anywhere else.

The first section derives from a tour in a hired car around Romania in 1998. It has to do with not knowing where you are, and noticing things which might later develop into glimpses of something. But the pieces in sections 2 and 3 at Poienile Izei, Mociu, and the second at Budeşti were also during this tour.

The second section stays in Maramureş, a mountain-ringed enclave in the far north of Transylvania against the border with Ukraine, which became the base of all subsequent visits through the generous hospitality of Ioan and Anuţa Pop in their house in Hoteni. The villages of the two valleys here, the Mara and the Iza, have a character quite distinct from the rest of Transylvania or anywhere else, most evidently relict, but also, as I claim, advanced, or at least exemplary. This is of course highly contentious in a world dominated by a materialism which regrets its own results.

For a directly opposed view based on roughly the same amount of experience in exactly the same place, see the TV film 'The Last Peasants' by Angus MacQueen (first shown March 2003). Roughly: that behind the pastoral glamour it is a place for the old and the dull; all the bright young things can't wait to get out and away from a life of poverty and toil. I don't altogether deny this view, but most places can offer major contrary versions of themselves and this wasn't the one we were looking for. We were looking for what held the place together rather than what was out to destroy it, in the hope that some things, not easily locatable elsewhere, might be unerasable. We didn't go there to be disillusioned; we can be disillusioned where we are. MacQueen's film agrees with me that most of those who do get out want desperately to get back.

Of course one worries about what's going to happen to the area, but so one does of most areas. I don't myself know an area where one doesn't worry about what's going to become of it, if it hasn't already.

The third section has pieces taking place in several different parts of Transylvania proper, including Hungarian-speaking villages of the centre and west, visited from Maramureş or passed through on the way there or back.

It should be added that in five years some of these places have changed considerably, especially as new non-traditional houses have sprung up everywhere, and the description "villages of wooden houses" is now only selectively valid. Tractors are replacing horse transport in some areas and lorry routes for forestry or quarrying are being driven through many villages, so that the very low ambient noise level of 'Quiet Pastures with a Small Thunderstorm' is in process of erosion. Many of these changes are themselves the result of the efficiency of the traditional agricultural system.

The great acceleration of these changes since this book was first published, and especially following Romania's entry to the E.U. in 2006 are briefly covered in the appendices, but it is difficult to keep up with the pace of change or to gauge the ambiguity of response.

Further ramifications of these original visits are in my poem sequence 'Sett Two' in *A Map of Faring*, Parlor Press (U.S.A.) 2005. An essay on a genre of Transylvanian music, 'Dawn Songs', is on my website, www.aprileye.co.uk

I

Arnota

First you go to the village of Bistriţa, the end of the road. The road turns to dirt at a bar among trees and ahead of you are the gates of a big 18th Century monastery now a school for mentally disabled children. There is a parked bus, men sitting around outside the bar, children come and go, sunlight scattered on the ground through trees. To get to Arnota (having asked) you advance towards the monastery gate and turn to the right in front of it, descending behind houses on dirt and stones to the little river that bypasses the village. An open space at the foot of the mountain littered with sticks and grass and parts of concrete conduits. The track fords the stream, and there is an old painted sign: "MÎNÎSTIRE" with arrow where it turns into a wooded cleft and starts climbing. There is to be four kilometres of this. In the lower slopes there are wooden fences alongside under trees, wooden houses behind them, people walking, always there are people walking on the roads, carrying wood and water, leading beasts, children looking up. Then more steeply into the mountainside gullies and ledges, up towards the quarries. The surface is just about drivable, with big potholes and water-channels, sudden areas of soft sandy soil which need to be taken at some speed, hairpin bends one after the other climbing the mountain-side. Twice we come round a corner and meet a personnel-carrier descending, heavy trucks loaded with people, slowly creeping back down to the village, for it is already past mid-afternoon.

The track, and the guidebook gave no warning of this, leads straight into the quarry site itself, with a barrier lowered across the road. A man appears at the door of a brick hut, I shout "Mănăstire!" and the barrier is raised, with a smile. We go ahead into an enormous lorry park, and stop, confused. The barrier attendant has walked out behind us and is shouting the Romanian for "left", and slapping his raised left arm. The message eventually reaches us and we locate a further track leading out from the left corner of the site, it is really the most enormous quarry. And this track is steeper than ever, we are crawling in first gear on a very rough surface with patches of exposed bedrock, three more sharp bends, to come close up to the top of the mountain by a metal fence, with a gate, and an old sign for the monastery fastened to it. We stop, get out and look around. The quarry stretches away below us, half of that side of the mountain removed, caterpillar trucks crawling around far below. But we have risen past that and the summit area itself is wild enough beyond the perimeter fence, bare rocky slopes with tough shrubs and small oaks, and small flowers springing from crumbled red rock, for it is spring. The wire gate is open and we drive on through it and curve up to a parking space by the monastery wall.

A very small monastery, just a perimeter wall and a central church. You walk through the gateway and the church stands there in grass with the wall round it. Near the gate and opposite there are rooms in the wall, but the rest of the perimeter is bare. That is, the living quarters are built up against the wall and form a part of it, with balconies and windows facing inwards into the enclosure. Whoever lives here eats and sleeps inside the wall. A white church, 17th century Romanesque. We stoop to enter and it's dark, the iconostasis and hangings dimly glittering, painted figures on the walls, carpeted floor… an old monk sitting on a chair, who doesn't intervene.

He waves permission to photograph. He sits and watches us, in case, for instance, we might attempt to enter the sanctuary. We peer: the saints recorded on all sides, the silver icons, the heavenly narrative mounting up into the blackened dome, we walk back out. We notice the porch frescoes and the carved door, and go out into the compound and stroll around. There is an area where vegetables are grown to the west of the church, and a cow beyond a wooden fence. There are undisciplined poultry at various points. To the east, behind the apse, a single washing line stretches from the church to a post, bearing a few items of monkish underwear and socks. There are two kittens running round on a ledge near the gate. There is no sign of a second inhabitant. It is quite warm in the late afternoon, the quarry sounds are distant, an even wind moves across the compound, stirring slightly the outside trees.

Where are we, and how does this place exist? The monk comes out and looks at his cow. He doesn't look like a monk but is one, old and slightly bent, and wearing a black felt cap and a brown gown. He is not interested in visitors, but he has nothing against them. He moves slowly to the gate and stops near a small pile of logs.

And what about the night, and what about the depths of winter? Who or what comes to this site then? In snow and blizzard and darkness, the trees threshing in the wind or standing frozen, living in the wall with a three-month store of fuel and food, alone, a candle under a crucifix in a wooden room in a stone wall – alone? is that right? – one church one guardian one cow? Scrupulous diurnal discipline, standing alone in the church on the top of the mountain with a candle at night reading the frescoes, saying the words. Who are the visitors then? – foxes, concerned novices who hike up from Bistriţa, buzzards, bears? Do bears amble along in the middle of the night and sniff at the closed gate?

The Brancusi Monuments
at Tîrgu Jiu

The guide-books say this is all the town has. All it has is what Brancusi gave it: a stone arch, an avenue, a stone table with ten stools round it and, on the other side of the town, a very tall and slender iron-clad column.

A square arch of limestone through which you enter an avenue cut through the trees of the town's park, with eggtimer-shaped (cross-shaped) stone stools marking its edges, leading on the far side of the park to a low circular stone table, the Table of Silence, with ten similar stools round it, just before a grassy embankment. If you climb the embankment you find the river, very wide here, a few factories and flats far away on the opposite bank. If you turn round and look back down the avenue towards the arch you are facing straight towards the Endless Column on the other side of the town, but you don't see it.

The arch (like the column) is a construct of motifs. Vertical lines turn to drape over vertically bisected circles, which if you have been told, writes of an intimate Platonic harmony proposed as the foundation of a new public structure, at the end of a war. The column, if you see it or if you know, over there beyond the buildings the other side of the railway, is a sign of ultimate belonging, the cross of "here" reaching into the sky. If you don't know, or can't see, you are left with the town.

I was perfectly happy with the town.

We got to stay in a monster ex-Party concrete hotel full of unused spaces and unlit stairwells. We got driven out of this in the evening by hunger, to circumambulate the town's big central space looking vainly for an eating-place (no one can afford to eat out in Romanian towns) but admiring the big public space free of traffic with people strolling around and little children on bikes, how the milder poverty promotes calm and safety. Then viewing a couple of closing coffee-bars, a half-stocked food store, buying a bottle of sweet red wine from a small shop and finding eventually a little pizza-place opposite the hotel, friendly and slow. And I had to admit I was rich here, who back home couldn't afford a thing. And being rich with nothing to buy restored me to my place.

We got back to open the window on the second floor and look out as darkness arose between the buildings below us, which seemed sparsely occupied or neglected, with unkempt gardens and orchards, the corvines in the treetops over Brancusi's structures making a hell of a row.

Next morning the habitual struggle with breakfast-language produced a sausage, at last. We were at tables to one side of a sombre, brown, unused ballroom with an unstocked bar, a television loudly on as always and an empty bandstand with a carpet on it. Everyone else was male and looked like a migrant worker. Behind where the last band ever played, the brown wall had a scattering of silver paper stars glued to it, rather tattered now, looking as if they had been cut out of chocolate wrappers with scissors.

But a bright morning sunlight that makes any poor town a good place, restored our energy. The Arch of the Embrace, the avenue again, the stone table vacant and silent as if waiting seventy years for the meeting which will settle all our differences. We follow Brancusi's instruction and walk back down the avenue under the arch and straight on through the town: past the hotel, across the town square and its half-stocked shops in vague morning movement; then a street of uncertain institutional buildings, to be diverted either side of a lumpy 19th Century church, and straight on again through the small inner suburbs with slightly rural houses, finally to step across the railway where the street ends into the other park, the other space. And there, straight in front, half a kilometre across long grass, the column.

The column is encased in scaffolding. A camp of temporary huts and large vans enclosed in a steel barrier spreads round its foot. Peering through the scaffolding reveals that the column is completely boxed in, and invisible. A multilingual notice explains that the column is being restored because it is suffering from rust. The restoring enterprise is based in Paris and financed internationally from western Europe. A message from places where we are always in search of reasons for spending money.

And what happens to Brancusi's schemes, his allegorical interventions, when you don't have any of his statements to hand or any of the art criticism in the world but stand in some fairly desolate Romanian town going about its inscrutable business on a mild morning with these forms and lines before your eyes, which are not so different after all from a lot of the forms and lines that appear before us in most places in the world, small town parks, trees, half-tended flower-beds, with desolate aviaries, straight-sided public toilets, lines curving or not over circles or mounting into the sky crossing each other… if you could see them? If you don't remember for instance The Kiss at Montparnasse you are mainly left with a vertically bisected circle and a Romanian park struggling in vain against nature. And it is always better not to be instructed, on what you are supposed to perceive. But to feed what you notice into a reservoir, somewhere behind the brain, of accumulating tokens, to be spent as needed.

But what you do see, that particular line curving to bisect that uniquely swelling circle in creamy travertine polished to something like the gloss of human skin… Diagrams of affection replacing the triumphs of a military arch, a new foundation of the state… I think these simple forms convince us that what we share at large is the very basis of what we are or hope to be.

Breakfast at Sibiu

The "pension" in the old town, a mass of red roofs tumbling down the hillside, didn't do breakfast. It did a quaint room on the second floor with a stag-at-bay tapestry on the wall, assorted house-clearance furniture, and a thin balcony onto more red roofs. There we sat in the evenings with cooked meats and bread and sweet red wine in an urban quietness rare where we come from, a city soundscape of footsteps and voices. We began each day by walking up to the town centre, on stones, under all the perched baroque houses to the café-bar in the main square, and sat outside in the warm May mornings. Never anyone much about, many signs of poverty and constraint.

By negotiating breakfast-language within, which was like a Manchester 1960s coffee-bar with a tile stove added, we got coffee, omelettes and sauerkraut (which came unasked) brought to the table. The sauerkraut was a reminder that Sibiu was a German town, as its architecture still is, and most of its street signs and official notices still bilingual, but the Germans have all fled.

Two little boys approached and stood by the table, silently asking for food. This was clearly accepted as normal by the proprietors and other customers. It was not seen as creating a problem. There were only a few other tables occupied, mainly drinkers getting started for the day.

We spared them half a bread roll each and the sauerkraut, which we pointed at to ask "Do you want this?" Yes, they wanted that. They scooped it onto the bread and went away.

A moment later I looked over to my left and saw them, they were about eight, sitting at a table facing each other eating the bread and the sauerkraut, and looking very happy, grinning radiantly at each other. They had achieved breakfast. And they never so much as glanced towards us, we were finished with: they had asked, we had given, it was ended. No sullen or resentful laterality: they focused on each other joyfully. The day was now before them. It shone on them.

I remembered a gypsy boy who pestered me in Satu Mare when I'd just arrived and had no Romanian currency, persistently at my elbow whichever way I turned, continuously talking, pleading – acting, a necessary acting – until he was content with some Hungarian coins worth next to nothing. And two hours later we met him again as we were crossing the town square and he smiled cheerfully at us and shouted "Hi!". No residue, no guilt, no resentment – normal life getting on with its business, necessity rather than desperation.

And I thought of the other beggars we'd met, in Bucureşti and Tîrgu Mureş, professionals, pushing truncated leg-stumps out onto the pavement, moving on crutches at other people's waist level, one of them so deformed I thought at first it was street theatre, and a gypsy girl walking on her hands at Huedin... And I'd asked our friends at Tîrgu Mureş, "There is a lot of begging, do you think it is necessary?" Yes, it is necessary.

And being necessary it is very hard, but doesn't leave a residue.

The Taragot on the Bridge at Tîrgu Lapuș

A bridge over a wide shallow river marks the end of the town centre. Needing to walk after a day's driving, we got out of our "motel" at the other end of town and strolled down the main street until we crossed the bridge. There was nothing else to do. Another deprived town centre, all its edges worn and dusty, its hotel abandoned, its shops half stocked, its restaurants a memory. We walked slowly, half crossed the bridge and paused before starting back, leaning against the parapet, sniffing the air, alert to what was happening on all sides as you are in a foreign place. It was a warm evening, a few people about as the light started to lessen, mostly coming in twos and threes towards the town centre, to linger outdoors there for the evening, in no hurry. They might buy a drink, they won't buy a meal. The river rattling under on the stones.

There was a strange musical noise on the other side of the bridge and soon afterwards a small man in a long dark coat and black hat could be seen emerging from the area of small bars beside the river and starting to cross the bridge. He carried a small suitcase, and every time he encountered someone he opened it and got out a clarinet or something like one, a quite long instrument of pale wood, and he played a short passage on it. People evidently ignored him or expressed disdain and he returned the instrument to its case and walked on. This happened twice. He was obviously neither begging nor drunk. He crossed the bridge and turned down towards an area of modern blocks of flats such as all Transylvanian towns have in legacy from state communism and its enforced population movements. We started to walk back but the clarinet sounded again. He was standing in front of an elderly working man in his shirt sleeves who evidently took an interest. The musician played for a while and stopped. His audience took the clarinet from him and examined it carefully, then handed it back. He played again and was listened to, with nodding. A few words were exchanged, he put the instrument away, they bowed slightly to each other and continued on their ways. There was no exchange of cash or cigarettes or anything. My sense was that the musician viewed his instrument and what he could do with it as a rare thing which he ought to show to anybody while it was still possible. It was a woody, breath-laden reed sound, and the melodic line was something which could only exist somewhere which had once been within earshot of the Ottoman Empire.

The Road

A long straight road with a railway running alongside, in northern Romania, parallel to the Ukrainian border. A series of small towns or villages about 8 km apart ending at a monastery: Rădăuţi – Horodnic – Gălăneşti – Vicovu de Jos – Putna. Open, windy countryside, farmed land, clouds passing over. A few gentle hills far off to the sides covered in patches of cultivation, those on the right probably in Ukraine, but the road straight and level. Road and railway running always side by side, across the countryside, through the scrubby town centres and the long linear villages, so extenuated that the end of one is never far from the beginning of the next, and there is never much distance without houses. One-storey wooden houses with fences round them, strung out along either side of the road. Houses on the railway side have the railway running past their gates, sometimes with planks or sleepers set between the rails so that a car or cart can gain access to the yard, sometimes nothing, you just step over the railway to your door. Always people on the road, walking, a few cars and pick-up trucks, a lot of horse-drawn carts, but above all people walking. Occasionally, between villages, road and railway exchange sides and there is a level crossing, a few lumps of cement set between the lines, very bumpy, to be taken in first gear, and no barriers, just an old sign saying: Watch out for trains. No trains this afternoon. Storks' nests on telegraph posts. Children with blond hair.

Storks' nests on posts. They peer down at you, you can see their eyes gleaming. They have a certain way of looking at you, as if they know exactly what you're up to, no wonder they were given the job of bringing babies.

When I was an infant, in the industrial north of England, they brought babies, and no one had ever seen a stork or had more than the faintest idea what it really looked like. And to the young kids who were told this it was a far more mysterious and wonderful thing than any baby, a strange big white bird floating in the blue-black starry sky of a printed book holding a cloth bundle in its beak. And here they are, in person as it were, standing in big woody nests on posts and roofs, bending their necks and peering down at you. And clacking their beaks, for it is the mating season. There are children everywhere.

Children, and people living in wooden houses going about their businesses. For ever and ever and ever.

II

Unchi

We notice on the second day at Hoteni that there is a third presence in the house. There is us, and our hosts, but there is also an old fellow around the place who minds his own business, looks after the chickens, and works in the fields. This is Unchi.

"That's my uncle," Geta explains. "He never got married, and when we asked him where he wanted to live, he said he'd like to live down here and look after the chickens and work in the fields, so that's what he did. He's all right at present, but I worry about what will happen when he's older and gets ill."

He's in his late eighties. He has a very regular weekday routine: early rising, chickens, work in the fields, chickens, church, read, retire. He moves around the place quietly, takes his meals in his own room which is on a back corner of the house, and we don't normally notice his comings and goings. He is small and somewhat stooped, in dull jacket and always a hat, but there are signs of originality: suddenly on a warm day he appears in something like a long striped green and yellow football shirt, and on a colder day in a thick pseudo-leather overcoat inscribed on the back with the letters TDK. This must derive from Popic's musical business. We have occasional dealings with him during the two weeks as best we can, concerning times, keys, weather, chickens… It's obvious that he's a friendly, shy, contented man.

"He never got married". But it says in the books that in this highly structured peasant society marriage and reproduction are of central importance, stressed and re-stressed in every ritual enactment, at birth, wedding and death, at every calendar node, that they are essential events to the mind-set of this society, and that to remain unmarried is a kind of disgrace, certainly a terrible failure, liable to make anyone a figure of fun or a despised outcast. But this is a contented old man whom everybody likes.

"He wanted to look after the chickens". But it says in the books that this is women's work which a man would never touch for fear of ridicule. It says that gender roles are strictly adhered to and confirmed in the cultural performances as integral to a male-governed society in tune with irrevocable cosmic order. He makes little clucking noises and knows each hen by name.

I don't believe the books. I think the cosmic performances are as much liberating as integrating, that they release you from this society as much as they confirm you in it. I think they are a kind of essential ornament, like a beautiful shawl wrapped round you which tells you you are not so poor and miserable, clothing the labourer in the fields in bright regalia.

Unchi is never around in the early evening or most of Sunday. "He's very religious, he's at the church every evensong and twice on Sunday, when he visits friends in the village between services. Every day when he's finished with work and church he goes to his room where there is no television or radio, he doesn't want them. He sits there and reads these religious books he gets from the Priest. Actually we think he knows every word of them by heart because sometimes he sits there reading without a light as night comes on until it's really dark, still turning pages…"

In the second year of our visits, having gathered that Beryl speaks "some Romanian" he casts aside all fine distinctions and suddenly, outside the front of the house on his way to the chicken shed, delivers us a forty-minute lecture on the history of the second European war.

He is often in sole charge of this house off the edge of the village, indeed most weekdays since Popic and Geta have to work in the town where they have a flat. You'd think it a very lonely existence, but we begin to understand how things work round here, that in the big quiet expanses of valley fields with wooden houses dotted around, there will always be someone who knows where Unchi is and what he is doing, that if he needs anything whatsoever he will go to the nearest house and ask for it, that if he were to collapse while working in the fields someone would be running over to him before you could count ten. You look at the valley and see a lot of distance, but really there is a lot of proximity.

Gypsy Neighbours

It was a feast day, and there were visitors. The feast was the "Tânjaua" or "First Ploughman" festival, a big affair involving the whole village in processions, ceremonies, frolics, dinners, and later a big song-and-dance show in a meadow outside the village, with attached market. Still referred to in some guidebooks as a "fertility rite". The visitors were from București, a group of four, successful shopkeepers formerly from this area, visiting for the festival. Big, well-fed, prosperous people, square in shape, full of talk about politics and hunting.

We were all sat round the table in the kitchen having lunch before going out to witness the events. A boy of about ten walked in the back door. He was from a gypsy family lower down the valley and he was begging, politely and modestly. He was also noticeably well dressed, in a bright and new-looking jacket, for it was a feast day. He did very well. Everybody, one by one round the table, gave him money generously, notes rather than coins; he was treated warmly, asked questions about himself, and left holding a piece of bread and butter with plum jam.

About the same time next day we were with Popic and Geta outside the front door waiting for a group of young Americans to arrive. A woman and two children walked through the gate and came over to us. She was small, dark skinned, greying hair, in an old printed dress. There were two little boys, one of whom was the boy who had come begging the day before but now in much poorer clothes, the other presumably a younger brother. The group just walked over and stood with us, nods, good-days, and the woman spoke a few words to Popic quietly.

This was obviously a concerted family effort at a second go, following the success of the previous day, as if they might be onto a very good thing here. But there was no pushing, no pleading, no lengthy explanations or tales, no patter, just a few words quietly spoken by the woman, and the boys just stood there. A hand was not held out. Equally obviously, this return to presumed rich pastures was not looked upon by our hosts as a thing to be encouraged. Nothing much was said by them either, a certain amount of shrugging of the shoulders, and getting on with things.

So she didn't get anything, but her importuning, such as it was, didn't meet with any anger or resentment, indeed there hardly seemed to be any denial, and nobody told her to go away. These are neighbours, you don't tell neighbours to go away. Your land is open to them: anyone who wants to get to somewhere beyond your garden will walk across it as long as there's a gate or a gap in a hedge, and would be expected to. And they didn't go away, they hung around with us, the boys staring at the foreigners, and she occasionally said a few words and was replied to. Not at a "respectable distance" either, but among us. I was expecting her to be told something like "Sorry, my dear, really nothing doing today, off you go", but it didn't happen.

They were still there when the Americans arrived, two young couples in a minibus with a Romanian driver, who parked and came over to us. Welcomes and introductions took place, and the gypsies stood there with us for all the world as if part of the household – which is what one of the Americans took them for and shook hands with her.

Then we went indoors and they drifted away, across the grass and through the door in the gate. And they went without any signs of disappointment or resentment. They went as if it was now time to go, so they went.

The Poor Couple

Geta is giving us a lift to Ocna to make a telephone call, in the old dormobile they use for getting the singers and instruments to gigs and tours. After we have driven up through the village there is a couple walking along the side of the road, and Geta stops ahead of them. "We must give them a lift," she says, "they are the poorest people in the village, and she is not well."

They are small and quiet. They get in behind us. They are obviously impaired, dazed, somewhat vacant, unfluent. They wear the local clothes in threadbare cast-off versions, his circular Maramureş straw hat brown with dirt, she in headscarf and worn jumper. They answer Geta's inquiries briefly, they never smile. They are told who we are but I'm not sure that it really registers, that whatever we are described as means anything to them. Geta drops them in the town square. They acknowledge my door-opening and a hand down with a numb reserve. I feel that they are grimly, quietly, all the time, struggling to be what persons are meant to be. They are not alienated or proud; they are wrapped in a permanent, solid, disappointment, that they do not exactly become what people are. They wander off together into the town.

They live in a house in the fields off the north-east side of the village. They have several children, some of whom are ill, they have no land and they have no money. It is difficult for either of them to get, or do, work. This is what constitutes "being poor" here: not having money, but also not having anything else either, any of the things that precede or supercede money. People help them; Geta's parents whose smallholding is on that side of the village, visit and help them. People take them packets of what surplus there is from time to time. There is a problem with alcohol and villagers are worried about the welfare of the children. The children will be noticed and helped but no one will intervene under authority. My sense of how this place works is that if the children really need to be away from the family house that's where they will be anyway, they will already have got there by then.

Because of queues we have to wait a long time in the post office, the small first room or foyer of which containing the telephone cupboards is permanently open. We sit on a bench. After about twenty minutes we look up and see her there, the poor woman, holding a printed document in her hand which is her entitlement to some money from the State, standing facing the closed position. It is nine o'clock on a Sunday evening. The closed office is obviously a terrible disappointment and completely incomprehensible. She can neither come nor go, she just stares at the closed counter, as if she is staring at herself, and can't do a thing about it.

The Bar at Breb

We walk from Hoteni to Breb. I sometimes find it very difficult to believe that I am really where I am. I am in Old Europe, I am in something not very far from what I would be in if I were in the rural narratives of Gogol or Turgenev, except that the aristocracy have been removed. Nobody seems to miss them. We're walking on a dirt road between cultivation strips and patches of woodland. There is a startling purple and yellow flower beside the track which we later find in Keble Martin's *Concise British Flora* as "common cow wheat", meaning that Britain also was once Old Europe, but not any more. Perhaps one of the essential conditions of remaining Old Europe is getting rid of the old aristocracy, and not letting in the new one, the people with the hungry money.

We enter Breb. There are wooden houses with big fences around them among the trees either side of the road above and below us, all different, each smallholding with its own tone to its décor, its own style in the carved gateways and eaves and verandas. We could happily stop and study any one of them for half an hour. But if we did this we'd probably be seen and invited in and given a three-course meal with home-brewed spirits at the very least, quite possibly resulting in a permanent relationship involving Christmas cards. If we want to get back before dark it is better to walk on. We view the exterior of the wooden church. We pass a water-driven fulling mill, the wheels stilled. It's very quiet everywhere because of the time of day and year, most people are out in the fields. We are in Old Europe and whatever threatens it at large, this late afternoon in Breb it gets on with its work.

We are hot and need a drink, where is the village bar? We escape a problematic person, and round a corner meet a girl of about seventeen walking towards us in the usual clothes: headscarf, blouse, dark flowered skirt.

She has just got off the bus from Sighet. We ask her where is the bar. She says Yes and leads us along with her. She says several times something we don't get but which seems to be a positive thing. She has come from the music school at Sighet where she is studying singing. Does she sing Transylvanian music? Yes, we think she says yes she does, and leads us through the village.

All you need is someone to take you in hand. Foreigners are like infants here. There are risks of unpropitious involvement, or of unwittingly violating custom, but someone will come along and take you in hand, and lead you through the labyrinth to a bar or goal. We have been in the most tensely ceremonious occasions, even a death-wedding, and someone has taken us in hand and led us by the arm and said without language, "Yes, come this way so you can see what is happening, it's all right, press forward up here with me to be close to the event…" And once you're taken in hand, you're there, you're part of it.

The bar is in the lowest floor of an old building in an open space away from the centre of the village. She doesn't just show us where it is, she gets a key out of her bag and unlocks the door and goes in and switches the lights on. She is the daughter of the "patron", it's her job to run the bar every evening when she gets back from school.

We've been to a lot of places before which look like Old Europe and which retain the streets and the masonry of Old Europe, but there has never been anybody living there in Old Europe. Which is to live with the generations as they turn over like a slow water-wheel. Which is to live without the felt need to surpass your parents. And no doubt to live in ever-threatening worry and relentless toil, but with something to stand on. But it is to live all this in a harmonic structure which also liberates you from it.

She sits us down and serves us. There is no Coke or Fanta available, which is bad news because the locally made soft drinks are coloured chemicals and sugar, and in big bottles, but we accept them. She would like to play traditional music for us on the bar's cassette-player; she brings out a box of cassettes but they have all been removed from their original containers and the local cassette industry never labels the objects themselves. So all she can do is keep putting them in the machine, a little portable, one after the other. We get modern ("gypsy") music every time. She gives up the attempt and sits smiling at us. Nobody else comes in, it's far too early.

We don't find much to say, but it doesn't matter. We don't have enough of the language to ask how it is, that a seventeen-year old girl can be alone in charge of the bar in a big village like this night after night, till midnight most nights, she says. The village bars such as we've noticed have more often than not seemed places to avoid. They are not part of the old village plan, which doesn't necessarily include an inn – travellers used to rely on traditions of domestic hospitality. They are usually in the village centre attached to the shop, classes of building introduced, along with clinics and Ministry of Agriculture offices, by the Communist regimes. Women seem not to frequent them, and most of the customers are the unlanded peasantry, labourers and gypsies. The alcohol consumption level is probably very high unless poverty forbids it, and we have seen burly workers just in from the fields sitting at tables drinking mineral water. But most villages seem to have at least one standard village drunk, with a marked tendency to buttonholing strangers and leading them by the hand. We can't ask her how it is that she can be a seventeen-year-old girl and run this place every night. And yet we understand it perfectly because there she is in front of us, smiling at us from behind the bar: there is obviously no problem. And that too is Old Europe, with its jittery amplified music and its low-quality soft drinks and its little fairy-lights strung across the ceiling… and a teenage girl can raise her head and walk in perfect confidence through the village late at night from the bar she runs to her home. Because everybody knows that she can.

We thank her with farewells and walk out, find the road and walk back towards Hoteni, suffering only lightly from the indigenous pop gas. The light is getting low and birds are moving to their roosts, but people are still working in the fields, hoeing, stacking hay, steadily repetitive hard work, all day long. Some of them stop and say hello to us, and ask where we're going. As soon as we tell them, everything is restored to confidence. "We are staying at Popic's house in Hoteni". "Ah yes, Popic, we understand." And they beam at us and we walk on.

The Walk to Ocna Şugatag

A track goes off to the left where the road takes a corner above the village. Even a small village like Hoteni has this ragged edge, this blurring into the fields, that a city has. An uneven row of five or six wooden houses on the left of the track, smaller and poorer than the houses in the village proper; these are people with one cow and a few geese. In front of the houses, areas of trodden grass with bushes and trees, merging into the open pastures, several horses wandering freely. A communal shadoof well, a flock of geese, some bits of radio noise from the houses.

A place that manages to survive on the edge of a place that manages to survive. I feel I should walk on tiptoe. There was a woman sitting on a bench outside her house with her cow next to her, gently singing to it. I couldn't think of any finer thing to do on earth.

The track goes on, over the brow, and dips into a small valley head with a lake at the bottom. Untidy grass and bushes. The town is already visible up the other side. As it descends towards the lake the track passes ruined shapes, I don't know what they are: tanks, conduits, or what they are made of: concrete, stone, grassed over, dim rectangles. Further down, on the left, a square brick-lined pit with stagnant water at the bottom full of creatures making a loud chirruping noise. It occurs to me that in Britain this structure would require (a) a metal perimeter fence (b) four large notices reading BEWARE OF PIT. The owners of this property accept no responsibility for loss or injury resulting from unauthorised entry... etc. (c) A sign reading: Site of special scientific interest, followed by a list of criminal offences. Near this we notice we are walking on a bed of sawdust for a few yards. This interests me rather more than the pit, because it means that this apparently disregarded track has in fact been thought about, and has received some practical attention to assist anyone who uses it, by dumping a load of sawdust over a place where a streamlet crosses the track, otherwise forming a mud-slide.

The lake is not natural but fills the excavations of a former salt industry, with small ochre cliffs on most sides. It is unfenced and here too there are no warning notices. Either it is not dangerous or people know it is dangerous. There are some young people swimming, diving from an overhanging cliff at the far side. But there's no one fishing, of course, it's a salt lake. Perhaps this is a land where people don't need to be told not to paddle in extremely deep water, or not to fish where there are no fish. It is a densely populated area, but by people who know where they are. Because they tell each other.

As we reach the lowest point, quite close to the lake shore, and turn away from it into the edge of the town on a wider track of spread stones, I don't know why but I start thinking about angels. There is a female grey-headed woodpecker on a small wayside tree. There is a boy leading a horse. There is a green-painted, dilapidated, shrine with closed door. There is a young woman slowly and with infinite patience manoeuvring an inhabited push-chair over the big stones of the road.

Ocna Spa

There is a "spa" at Ocna Şugatag. It consists of a hotel and swimming-pool complex on the main road north. Ocna is really no more than a cross-roads village; there is at the most one parallel street each side of the main road running north-south. Most of the housing is distinctly rural: bread ovens in the yard, a few beasts, etc. But the central square is quite large with town-like modern buildings, smart by local standards, and a stone church in the middle. It was a Hungarian foundation for the mines and so never a clustered wooden village like those that surround it, and it remains the administrative centre of the mini-region.

So the spa stands on the main road out to the north. The usable feature for hovering visitors is the bar, which is in an annexe to the hotel on the first floor, overlooking the swimming pools from its large veranda.

It is rarely boring to sit in a bar in Transylvania. What is the man we were introduced to two days ago as a "priest" from Vişeu, but who doesn't dress as one, doing here conversing in a business-like way with a woman at one of the tables, and why does he keep moving around mysteriously, exiting normally then reappearing through the back door of the bar which looks like a staff entrance? We shall never know, but he greets us heartily and excuses himself for being so "busy".

It is September, sunny and quite warm but nobody much around, a few off-season Romanian visitors, mostly quite elderly, to be seen pottering in the grounds of the hotel from time to time. The bar also is quiet, except for the table next to us, which contains seven or eight villagers. They too are elderly, five of them women, and clearly distinguished as the old style of "peasant" with their headscarfs, leggings, home-made clothes etc. They are drinking big glasses of draught beer and compared with everyone else they seem small, rounded and compact. Above all they are lively and happy, full of talk and curiosity, prattling on to each other, and they keep catching our eyes, smiling and nodding repeatedly.

They become very interested in three people, the only people using the circular swimming pools below us, a man and two women of fifty to sixty in swimming clothes who are lazing in the thin sunshine on the edge of the pool. All three are corpulent. The two women spend most of their time lying on pool-side benches; the man mostly sits but occasionally enters the pool, then climbs out and goes to a shower which is just behind them, and returns to sit on a bench.

The villagers find this trio very amusing. They look at them, laugh, drink, look back at them, laugh, comment to each other, look again, shake their heads, giggle, laugh. All of them, men and women alike, agree that this spectacle is really very funny. It might be the near-nudity, the man's swimming trunks almost invisible under his over-nourished belly, the exposure of such fleshliness… it might be the activity or lack of it: lying in the sun, immersing yourself in water, both ridiculous and pointless activities. I can't be sure what it is.

But the villagers are killing themselves laughing. The more they drink and talk and the more they look the more they laugh until they approach helplessness. This is really the funniest thing they have ever seen. This is the funniest thing in the world.

The Bar at Călineşti

The bar at Călineşti had a young man in it who was more than drunk, he was also mentally disabled, and the manner in which the other men controlled him and kept him out of mischief was exemplary.

It was a very small bar, a wooden shed down by the bridge with a counter and four tables. Like most bars it had a girl in charge, and there were three men sitting at a table with beers. It was mid-day and hot, we needed mineral waters and coffees, we got them and sat down. The men behaved exactly as we would have expected: nod, exchange good day, leave us alone and not show curiosity, until I looked over to them again and saw a young man's face looking straight at us with a big grin. This was unorthodox. "Hello," I thought, "here comes trouble." Next thing he was beside us, bending over us, hanging onto the back of one of our chairs, grinning and talking away in a broken, minimal way which showed his condition, but with great enthusiasm. We did our best, not having a clue what he was saying or intended, but knowing he wouldn't be asking for anything.

The other two men continued to mind their own business, but kept an eye on us all the time. They weren't apprehensive, they were merely in charge. They were satisfied as long as neither party showed signs of annoyance. They called him Mihai. When they reckoned we'd had enough they called him over, "Hey Mihai, come back here you [...]." He was back and forth. He wasn't a threat but he monopolised attention and wasn't in good control of his own movements, it would have been easy to be apprehensive. They treated him like a favourite dog, wagged fingers at him, sat him down, got him another drink, let him roam. He was back with us again, fascinated by us, sometimes just staring in our faces, sometimes trying very hard to convey something which to him was very straightforward. They smiled at us, raised eyebrows, threw the occasional comment to Mihai to restrain him a bit and eventually one came over, and neither pulled nor pushed but guided him, arm on his shoulder or waist, back to their table. Like someone leading a horse.

As we left we said good-bye to them as you should but didn't thank them, almost did but felt it was not quite right to. Mihai of course followed us, held onto the car door and communed with the driver, me, and I think I was beginning to catch on to the local methodology of Mihai-control which was basically calm reciprocation with uninterrupted flow of any action he might otherwise interrupt. He was happy enough certainly, and not giving up. The other two were outside the bar, with their bottles, watching us casually from the doorway. They called him back, but he rebounded. And suddenly there was another man by the car, a big farmer-looking kind of person full of indulgent grin, who said nothing. He just tucked Mihai's head under his arm and walked him away.

What's it about? I asked as we drove away. My mind was full of contrary images from a highly institutionalised country. Instructors, therapists, managers, in white coats or not, clinical sessions, permanent removal from family, small room in big modern building with bed chair and desk, video observation day and night, locked doors, reports on progress... Or possibly being chucked into "the community" to fend for himself without income in a back-street jungle. Here he got drunk, but lived somewhere, and was handled with virtuoso kindness. What's it about? It's about knowing somebody from birth.

The Oldest House in Budeşti

1

I thought in Budeşti I was seeing a new way of living in these villages. The man had a job in the metal mines over the hills at Cavnic, and travelled there every day in his car. He wasn't a miner, he was careful to add: probably a technician or office worker. But he also had his village function: he worked the family's land, and as his communal specialisation he provided the village abattoir. Thus being shown again round the buildings of a smallholding: the family house, the kitchen garden, the one-cow byre and so forth, there was also the small clean butchery room with chains and hooks hanging from the ceiling. And the summer kitchen was more modern and bright than usual, and off it, the most unexpected thing: a bath-room, with bath.

Inside the house the tone was less ceremonious than usual. It was not required of us to take a three-course meal with fire-water. A quick coffee appeared. We have been here, they told us, for countless generations, parent upon parent receding into an unknown past, the son getting married and building the new house in the father's yard again and again. And they had, it seemed, kept that, and moved ahead of it. There was no hint, in the unfolding of these multiple professions, of any strain on time or capacity, it seemed it was no problem to run the smallholding the abattoir and the job in the mine simultaneously. Employment in modern Romania can be very casually organised and rarely provides a real living wage. In the cities it has to be multiplied in the attempt to survive and the situation worsens every year; in the villages it might be a useful adjunct to an independent resource.

But the brightest thing of all was Ileana, who was thirteen and had found us wandering in the village as an opportunity to speak English. Since 1990 English has been the first foreign language taught in the schools, so that there is now a generation of pre-adolescents lurking in most villages waiting to take an English-speaking person home. She was our interpreter: she explained, guided, negotiated, she made grammatical mistakes and lost her vocabulary, especially when asked to translate specifically, but shone like a torch of youthful intelligence and unselfconscious charm. When she spoke to you she looked you straight in the eyes.

What, I thought, is the future of this brightness? Can the village structure of Old Europe, so rich in ornament, do anything but suppress it into drudgery? Does it have to get out of the villages? And what is "out" into Romania but failed urbanity, dismal squalid and polluted environments where people can't earn a decent living and fall to despair? Wouldn't it be better to stay here, wouldn't it be better to get as far away as possible, like Brisbane, or Cape Town? And think of that, think of launching out into the wide world with this basis under you, the moral world-vision of a real community consolidated over centuries which you carry round everywhere with you in your dealings and your care, and constantly return to.

Ileana is not nervous or over-excited by the sudden incursion of three foreigners for whom she is responsible, she is simply engaged in the occasion. What she doesn't understand or can't manage is just that, nothing more. She is ashamed of nothing, not her dirt-paved village or her slaughterman father or her faltering English, they are all set there as they must be, as things are in Old Europe. The old village gives her this, we know, we've seen it before in many children. But how does it translate through a whole life? Suddenly she says, "Would you like to see the oldest house in the village?"

2

As we walk out of the yard into the village street it is beginning to get dark. We walk along the main street on rough ground, the encroaching darkness blends with the earth of the road and this coupled darkness spreads into the air and the buildings and the people. It is a warm evening and people are out in it, everywhere, no lights at all, warm darkness all round us, people are shadows. They're in clusters seated on the benches of the yard gates, she calls to them, they know her, she tells them what we are, they call greetings, dark shapes sitting talking under the fence. Shadows pass by, one of them leads a horse. The stream chatters alongside on our left, little white flashes where it tumbles over stones, the road accompanies it up through the village. A clump of figures standing talking by the bridge, marked by the white patches of parts of the women's dresses. High up a side road the soft light of the big arched windows of one of the bars. More shadows move around us, clomping boots on hard earth, across and along our course, shadows about their evening business, the village is out in the night spaces. It's a big place but they all know her, all the shadows know her and accept her progress. We get over to where the village vale narrows and the stream is louder, with another bridge, a slightly lit bar on the right with fairy-lights strung up and many people round it, but no great noise, just talking voices and shadows moving around, filling the evening.

3

Over the bridge and higher up it seems lighter. Ileana precedes us into a wooden house with a few outbuildings on sloping ground. She returns to beckon us in. The threshold is a heap of rocks by which one gains the small veranda and through the door. But inside it's not a house, it's a wooden shell containing two huts. That is, we enter and are in a short wide corridor with a door to the left and another to the right, but up above us is the steeply pitched shingle roof, bits of dim sky showing through it. It's like standing in a big barn, and on each side is a small flat-topped wooden hut with things piled on top of it, the two rooms of the house.

Inside the one on the left is a small old woman sitting on a chair, a relative of Ileana's. She is perfectly happy to be visited without showing any excitement. She indicates things of possible interest, the old oil lamp not yet lit, the icons and old photographs on the wall, the round storage bin with a leg of pork in it, and her one book, a damaged almanac of about 1930. Everything is sparse, wooden, dark. Chair, table, bench, bed, stove, bin. Two small dark windows. She is happy for us to poke around her room, and takes us, as if outside, to see the other room.

The other room is even smaller and contains a bed and a stove. Left alone in it for a minute when the others turn back, I try to think what it would be like to sleep in this room. A small bed cornered against stove and wall, covered in rough dark textiles. To sleep there boxed in wood, in a tiny hut inside a barn and all those rural shadows outside, and the weather and the night sky… Rich wood and wool odours, earthen floor. You could do a lot worse, for sleeping.

The old lady says she is happy to live in this old house except that the big roof is in bad repair and in the winter a lot of water comes in. If Ileana stays here, will she "end up" like this, small old woman cradled in the locality, boxed in wood and wool? But with more than one book, and telling stray visitors she is on the whole happy to live in this old house, but saying it in English French or German… Or will this be a place to return to, and if so, who keeps it running while you're away?

As we walk down her steeply sloping enclosure there is another old woman coming very slowly up the path beside the fence. "Oh," says Ileana, "this is her mother." I have a momentary semi-comical vision of her mother coming up behind and a whole string of each others' mothers processing towards the house through centuries… We exchange courtesies and she speaks of arthritis.

Finally Ileana takes us to see one of the churches. The woman who holds the key happens to be walking down the road with a cow. It is too dark now to see almost anything inside it. In the graveyard Ileana points out the stone tables. One of the strangest things in these villages, where almost everything is made of wood, is that they contrive to have big stone slabs lying in the churchyards, old and pitted, megalithic, supported just a few inches off the ground. Each one belongs to an old family of the village and at certain occasions they will all squat round it and eat off it, as when honouring the dead on All Souls' Night, with candles. Rough, massive, things, which seem to anchor the families to the place by sheer weight, and glow at night. "This one here," she says, "this is ours."

The New Widow in the Churchyard

In most villages, the wooden church was by no means evident; you had to seek out your way there. It was somewhere in among the wooden houses and fences, to be reached by asking and venturing. The villagers themselves when they wanted to get to it just seemed to head straight for it, opening the gates of other people's yards and passing through them as necessary. If you asked you were likely to acquire a guide, who dropped everything he or she was doing and led you where you wanted to go and showed you what you wanted to see, and didn't expect anything in return.

At Budeşti it was a young man, a wrought iron worker we think he said, in one of the strange rimless round hats they wear in the region, whose dog had barked and so he took us under his wing and led us through several yards across mud-patches and through gates until we descended into the churchyard. And again one of those extraordinary sculptural edifices standing in long grass.

He hadn't got a key to it, but he was proud of it, it was a "national historical monument" and it was in his village. We stood at the west end gazing at it and as we moved round to the south became aware of a woman sitting on the bench that almost encircled the church under its overhanging roof, weeping. "This woman," the guide explained, "is very sad." She was about 45 with a quite gnarled round face, wearing the widow's headscarf that we'd seen so many women wearing in the streets of so many villages, but wearing it anew. "This woman's husband," the guide said, "died two days ago." And this, I thought, must be what you do in a place like this if this is what happens to you. You go down to the old church and sit on the bench, for how long, I don't know, how many hours, days, perhaps nights… You claim a solitude in which to donate yourself to the moment in all your hatred of it, knowing somehow, that this is how you work your way through it, and return to your life. Is this what you do?

Aware of these sightseers she became slightly animated and got up and turned aside from us and stood awkwardly in the grass, snuffling and shaking her head. Tears flew from her into the grass. As we moved round that side of the church, Beryl put an arm round her shoulder for a moment. We all bowed our heads involuntarily as before an icon.

The roofs of these things are made of oak shingles and rear above you like enormous waves.

Entering the Upper Iza Valley

Out of Sighet on the main road east, past the only new building, a hotel, clean concrete standing in weeds, full of water closets and entirely suitable for the new business and the new tourism and the new antiques trade which are eventually going to erase these places, if they don't erase themselves before they get the chance.

The road runs up the valley of the river Vişeu close to the edge of vast mountain forests which are the basis of the local economy. Somewhere along here there is still a steam railway which takes forest workers up into the mountains at seven o'clock every morning, past, I'm told, sometimes, bears drinking in the streams, and the rare sighting of lynxes.

You've hardly left the town when the next "village" starts, a mass of one-storey houses, some in the old wooden construction, more of them breeze-block and tin roof, all of them poor. It's called Tisa, becoming Bocicoiu Mare, then Rona de Jos (lower) then Rona de Sus (upper) but for the most part you'd hardly notice, the houses rarely stop, the road gradually climbs, the great valley full of poor housing heads slowly for the mountains.

The idea is to turn off onto a track through the village of Ruscova which leads to a remote mountain village, Poienile de Sub Munţe, inhabited by Ukrainians and described as very beautiful. We do this: the track is a road, not an easy one but a road, full of holes, the village is endless. Kilometres pass and we are still among houses on a road, and it's past three in the afternoon. There's nothing "rural" in sight, neither is there any industrial concentration, any obvious factory or centre. There are big stacks of trunks and logs in spaces between the houses, many of which have transportable sawing frames parked outside them – people make a living by taking them to where they're needed, a house being built or repaired. And people walking, as always, men women and children everywhere, not in that concerted "going home from work / school" way I remember in the streets of northern England in the 1940s – the only thing around here to remind me of that is the daily return of the beasts from the pastures – but an unregimented movement in all directions, in no hurry, stopping and talking, sitting outside the bar... Not then industrial in the western hierarchic mode, but still industrial, still thronging, urban, hanging on money. Waiting, perhaps, for the new multinational presence which is going to rationalise this throng into unidirectional observance, perhaps ready for that, in a form of poverty, a hanging-around without direction kind of poverty, which only that can offer to relieve. All the houses look in bad repair, the people's clothes look worn, the very air feels dusty and used.

After 10 kilometres we have had enough of this. Progress is slow, the mountain village still far away, it's getting late. We abandon the idea and turn round, and go back slowly through the whole scene again for another hour – unchanged, everyone still on the move – back to the main road and on up the valley. We go on through similar places to Moisei, where we turn onto a minor road to the right curving up the valley side, which is not high, and over into the top of the Valley of the Iza, which runs parallel to the Vişeu, to follow it back down towards Bîrsana and Ocna, and something happens.

Most of the terms for which seem wrong. Like saying we moved back in time, because quite possibly we moved forwards. Like saying we moved into a pastoral, because quite possibly we moved into a reality.

No more than glimpsed. The rich greens and whites of the vegetable garden, where the small river flows past the smallholding. The undertree light of the small orchards. The valley slopes covered in cultivation strips with tall lumpy haystacks standing all over them. Everywhere, clarity. People bending over the work of tending, women in wide black skirts and head scarves, men in white shirts. Wooden farms with decorated entrances to their yards, wooden churches on knolls. The very possibility of remaining self-sufficient, of just about managing, with very little help from the town, and that at a high rate, but in circles of light.

And on down the Iza Valley, which is, almost, a linear city of wooden houses 20 kilometres long. A linear city with the fields on either side reaching to its heart.

Poverty is a complicated thing. There are havens and chapels in it, as well as doors. There are rooms with pictorial walls, and yards where people sing and dance. There are pits of despair but also ceremonies of thanksgiving. And there is the working percept which is in touch with the human condition at its clearest, where the everyday habitation shows exactly what we are, wholesale and outright. And shows, in its physical motions its artefacts its trappings its earth-stained toil, what the business worker knows as an inward, concealed and incomprehensible melancholy, a despair for which there is no reason. Here the reason is carved on the door of the stockyard, and hung on the beams of the family space. And shines from the small river onto the vegetable patch, under the orchard trees, up to the mortal watershed.

The Last Working Narrow-Gauge Steam-Powered Forestry Railway in Europe

The previous evening, at the woodyard, they said to be there by six, and bring food for the day. The woman at the hotel said, "They always say six but nothing ever happens until seven or eight." But we got there before six.

The ticket office was closed because the woman who sold the tickets hadn't arrived yet. The only other person there, an elderly German in shorts with a rucksack, said, "I'm not waiting around here" and marched off among the railway lines and rolling stock. We followed him along the side of a long train of empty transporter wagons to a personnel wagon and a hissing locomotive. We climbed on board the wagon. It had a roof or canopy but no sides or windows and held about 20 people. It was already almost full but we found a double seat facing forwards. As soon as we had got ourselves in and sat down there was a great noise and it slowly moved off.

Something had happened to the processes of time. It was not yet fully light. A train was being pulled by a steam locomotive out through the long suburbs of a Transylvanian town, up a big valley. Slowly, at about human trotting pace, on a single track between fencing, the train trundled on past houses and kitchen gardens, alongside and across dirt streets. The houses were low, most of them made at least partly of wood, with oilskin or shingle roofs, each with attached orchard and vegetable patch, quite densely spread on the valley floor. There were hardly any lights showing, but that didn't mean people hadn't started their day yet. Everything was submerged in semi-darkness, infused with shadow.

The train went past again, as it did every morning. The engine made the deep rhythmic noises of its kind, and puffed out steam and a sweet smelling wood smoke which wafted back over us, with occasional red sparks floating round our heads. I caught a deep sense of European fate, of people bound to a structure without inhering reward, resigned to subjection, and disposable when it came to political crises. The state power-centre was very far from here, but its forces seemed to inhabit the morning darkness, its hand hovered over everything and might or might not go into action today. At the same time the smoke and noise took me back for a moment to my own 1950s. I was about twelve years old, haunting the station platforms and shunting yards of south Manchester holding a notebook. It was over in a flash. The dim first light also meant that there was a war on, which we might be escaping by this transportation to the high forest region. The low houses crowding the valley base were permanently under threat. There was a church on the other side of the valley across the river, with a bright light in its wooden tower. The river was wide and shone silver.

The locomotive: 0-6-0T, made in Hungary 1910, still hoarsely puffing its way out of the town nearly 100 years later, pulling about 20 empty transporter wagons, which are to receive felled tree trunks from the vast forests that stretch away in the mountains towards Ukraine, and one personnel carrier containing passengers and an official. We were on the bank of the river, and had not yet quitted the town when the first stop was made for refuelling. It took at least twenty minutes, a gang of three passing long pieces of axed wood from a track-side stack into the covered wagon behind the engine. At least half the passengers got off and hung around, until the whistle blew to collect them and we moved off again. We were to continue for 50 kilometres up the wooded valley of the River Vaser, with 15 such stops for various reasons, and it was to take half the day before we started the return journey. The valley is big and high, curves this way and that, and occasionally narrows, only once to what you would call a gorge, which we crept through on ledges and through tunnels. There are no dramatic vistas, it is for the most part a uniform large-scale forested valley which just goes on and on, and we follow it one side or other of the river, as if to the end of the earth.

The passengers were mostly Romanian families, plus a few of the determined, committed and undemanding people who reach this area as "tourists". They tend to wear very practical clothing. Also several elderly German men who spoke Romanian and so were probably revisiting Saxons, and two serious looking Czechs with rucksacks and tents. There were two young men, steam-freaks, whom we hardly saw because they spent more time off the train than on it, being obliged to film it on every bend or whenever a viewpoint was offered and so were constantly leaping off, running ahead, filming and jumping back on. At the speed we went it was easy to get on board in passing. But we also had a comedian among us.

The main feature of a Romanian two- or three-family group situated close to us, was a short plump man of about 40 with a very round face, a moon of a face, and straight thin black hair, sitting with his back to the engine, who kept the whole group entertained continuously. He sat there holding a two-litre plastic bottle of ţuică, and talked. Whatever he said provoked laughter in the group, sometimes extended and uncontrollable. We didn't know what he was saying but the whole act was thoroughly professional. He held himself quite stiffly, the voice under control, rather thin and tight, penetrative. I think a lot of it was ironically imitative of socially narrow styles, perhaps of his own milieu, but some of it seemed straight, pointed, rhythmically climactic. The way of passing the journey was to feed him opportunities. By the time they got off, for they were going to spend the night at some "cabins" about two-thirds way up, the bottle was empty, having been liberally passed round the entire personnel of the wagon, including the guard or conductor, but the greater part of it consumed by himself. The last 5 kilometres of their journey found him and two other men leaning against the back rail of the wagon loudly singing popular Romanian songs. These mountain valleys are noted for bears and even rarer animals, which is what a lot of people come up here for, hunters or the opposite of hunters, but this lot was focused entirely inwards; if there'd been a line of five brown bears standing by the track playing banjos they wouldn't have noticed.

And a conductor, or guard. A thin active man in a kind of uniform, including a peaked leather cap, his face marked by the smile of a wide mouth and a constant alertness in the eyes. He took our fares, quietly amused at our request for a "return", and was in charge of everything all day long. He supervised all operations and staff, kept an eye on the passengers, dealt with eventualities, moved around the wagon chatting in Romanian or German, joined the comedy audience for a while, and communicated with the driver by a code of whistles whenever necessary. He was under no constraint of regulations, and stopped and started the train as and when he thought necessary (a German tourist has gone for a pee in the bushes and is in danger of missing it, for example). He worked, or was active, the whole day through from six in the morning to seven in the evening, if not longer, never had a break and never ate, and never seemed tired.

So this long slow train with this mixed crew at its head of rowdies and contemplatives, screaming with laughter or mesmerised by the tree-coated valley sides and the river always beside us, puffed and hissed and snorted its way up into the mountains. And although we had left the town behind, it was still with us in the trees and rocks, in the milky water of the river, in the very air. Its slowness, its low income, its makeshift, its beggars and its cheerful souls shouldering the daily burden of inadequacy. And over the town was suspended the state. The blue sky covered a great uninhabited massif unable to escape the town's melancholy or the state's suspicion. So we went quite plaintively on for all our enjoyment.

We stopped at five "stations" which were permanent logging camps: Cozia, Bardău, Botizu, Făina, Valea Barbei, duly named on rail-side huts. Here wagons were dropped off to be loaded with trunks and picked up on our return journey, and the tender was re-stocked. At one such place three men were engaged in splitting sections of tree-trunk with sledge hammers and wedge to make the arm-length pieces for the locomotive. It took them about twelve minutes to reduce a piece of trunk standing upright in front of them to a heap.

There were always people around at these places, workers, mostly not looking very busy, or if on their way somewhere, on it slowly. They were utilitarian places without a trace of decor. A building or two in concrete if big, but otherwise wooden, in constricted open spaces among the trees. Stores of trunks and boughs. Not a trace of "peasant culture". Most of the men, for they were all men, looked like hard specimens, dark skinned, tough wiry bodies in compendia of old working clothes, boots, normally a hand-axe tucked in a belt. They looked a good deal grimmer than most of the men hanging around in the town, which is saying something. They stood watching or ignoring the daily train, some of them attending to it as necessary, paying scant attention to the coach load of "visitors" at the front. And sometimes we passed them, alone or in groups of two or three, walking along by the railway. Set, unsmiling faces, solitaries. They were obviously very poor however much they worked. And some of them travelled with us for various reasons; there were normally three or four workers on our carriage or nearby wagons. They were needed for loading and unloading and for eventualities. In several places the constant uphill gradient became steeper and the locomotive couldn't manage it, its driving wheels spinning as the steam mechanism raced, and the train halted. Then the guard and two or three others had to jump onto wagons at several points down the train to turn on their individual screw brakes, otherwise the train would have rolled backwards out of control. Then the train had to be split and taken up a half at a time. They threw track-side gravel under the wheels of the engine to help it get a grip.

They sat with us but didn't join us. They seemed acutely aware of their distance from us, didn't speak, didn't look at us except rather quickly and nervously, nor at the forest, but stared ahead waiting for the next task. They accepted a swig of țuică with thanks but it in no way unfroze them. Neither did they sit with each other. If there were two on our vehicle they were at far ends of it. Solitaries. One of them seemed obsessed with water. Every time the train stopped he walked over to the river and waded in it, and also drank water a great deal, filling has plastic bottle from springs whenever possible. These workers were like details from old Russian novels. Intimate knowledge of the behaviour of wood, ability to handle it in its massive raw forms, the experience and alertness to act in a team when an enormous tree trunk comes sliding fast down a gully, how to construct a wooden hut single handed in a few day, what to do when a bear approaches... Forest spirits and television game shows might have been equally within their repertoires.

At one point a bulldozer had to be loaded on, at another an excavator, to be carried from one stopping-place to another, for we also stopped at places with no buildings at all, where gangs were working in the forest. Both machines were driven up steep ramps hardly wider than their own tracks onto a flat wagon. Usually it took four or five attempts. They seemed to be climbing into the sky until they suddenly keeled forwards and crashed onto the floor of the wagon. This involved all available workers as helpers, drivers, advisors, witnesses.

Buildings other than forestry were rare. Higher up there was a quite big and well maintained unmarked house some distance away which I presumed to be border police or army. There was one smallholding near the track quite high up, no more than five small tilled fields, with its own tiny halt. There was a deserted house miles from anywhere with its exterior wall facing the track covered in erotic religious murals. And the minimal "resort" where the Romanian comedian and his families got out, or fell out, to spend the night. "He'll be having a long sleep now" someone said. A meadow or at least a space free of trees, a building, the river, and some small wooden cabins, somewhere. On the return journey the place seemed deserted.

There was a junction. Two valleys met, two rivers joined, two railway lines joined, we took the left over a bridge. The mountains didn't seem to get bigger, they just seemed to go on for ever, as did the river, which never seemed to get any smaller — shallow, full of milky water riding over stones. Occasional pools where weirs had been constructed from logs, the water curving over them in a pattern like corrugated cardboard.

To the end of the earth, still held in the hands of the town. To the end of the journey, though not to the end of the line. We halted nowhere in particular, with a siding, and a presumed forestry building not far away. The line continued ahead of us curving as the valley curved to the right. The locomotive went on alone round this curve and out of sight, it was never evident why, hotly pursued by the two enthusiasts. The river flowed beside us as always. We got out onto scrappy ground with electricity posts and no real growth, mainly stones and sparse grass, trees inhabiting the lateral slopes as if nothing else ever had or could. The end of the earth was undistinguished — there was nothing to see or do but to sit by the river and eat the packed lunch we'd been warned to bring. The end of the earth belongs to the state.

The end of the earth is the state. The desert, the stony mountains of Greece, the ice, the great barrier that encompasses produce. Nowhere, where No Name lives.

The locomotive returned and hitched itself to the other end of our wagon, now the only one left. The whistle was blown to assemble the passengers and we were off again, coasting down all the way back, stopping many times, to collect loaded wagons, fill bottles at mineral springs, other reasons. The engine, which had needed at least six loads of chopped wood coming up, needed none going down. The front of the boiler was before us, the old machine hissed, swayed and rattled as it rolled easily down. No more of the thunderous chugging that got us up. The track, looking back, was full of little kinks and wobbles, and grass was usually growing between the rails.

At the big valley junction a horse and cart was waiting for us with three men, who started loading white sacks onto an empty wagon, first laying leafy larch branches under them for protection. Cheeses, from mountain shepherds, on their way to market.

The guard had less to do and sat talking with the passengers a lot, mainly the group of Germans, and they got involved, obviously, in one of those extended, serious, and informed discussions on political and historical matters which most populations other than the British indulge so readily. He also pointed out things of interest as we passed by, such as big tunnels excavated in the sides of the gorge in quite inaccessible places, presumably by the state, as is the habit of states, always needing somewhere to hide something. The great Nowhere land followed us back to the town as it started to get dark again.

But it had been a hot day and we found some distance before the terminus that our way was impeded by work gangs repairing track which had buckled in the sun's heat. The halt was long, and when we went on we went extremely slowly, until on unaffected track. It happened again just as we entered the fringes of the town, above the broad river, which had children playing in it here and there, mostly in the middle of it. Some of the scattered, then compacted, small houses were busy, some showed lights, people sitting on the verandas, some proved to be bars with small groups sitting outside under lanterns – refuges, whatever from. The guard hung over the side of the train and dropped a packet of something, perhaps cheese, into the arms of his son as we passed his house. Then many stops to drop off the loaded wagons, and finally we rolled gently into Vișeu woodyard and halted. A few farewells, nothing much, the visitors ambled off towards their parked cars or walked into the town. The guard was still working, busy with something behind another line of wagons, perhaps getting tomorrow's train ready. When did the guard ever eat?

When he got home, perhaps at about 9 o'clock after putting the locomotive to bed and walking the kilometre up the track to his house, then he relaxed. And us, over-fed, over-spending, living too long, time on our hands, us unneeded persons, how we envy that relentless toil moving at its own pace, wanting only what it needs. How we envy that hunger.

Two Beggars

a) Little Girl with the Blue Dress on

A young girl in a blue and white dress. The first we noticed was not so much her appearance, but that something was tugging hard at the third finger of Beryl's left hand in the attempt to remove the ring on it. We looked, and there was a young girl in a blue and white dress walking alongside us earnestly and openly trying to steal the ring, without so much as a good-day. She must have been observing us as we walked slowly along the main street of Vişeu and planned a grab and run, but the ring was tight. When we perceived this and stopped her she showed mainly resentment at being interrupted, and far from running away, she stood in front of us and moved instantly from thief mode to beggar, but in terms of demand rather than request. She was about twelve, had dark skin and frizzy hair and a sharp, active face. The dress was so much a little-girl's dress, it was a cheap little-girl's dress with rudimentary flounces and frills, it wasn't gypsy wear and she seemed quite alien to it. She spoke loudly, incessantly and stared defiantly. She wasn't taking No for an answer. The coins we gave her, admittedly amounting to very little more than nil, were unacceptable and she flung them into the street. We didn't get a word she said but it hardly mattered. She was saying "Don't give me that worthless shit". The inclination to give her more was countered by her own aggression and tenacity. A somewhat higher sum was accepted but it didn't stop her performance and we made for the hotel. She clung to us relentlessly, and as we passed through the hotel's door she reached the pitch of striking Beryl in the back with her clenched fists and even then didn't give up but followed us down the corridor until intercepted and ejected by the staff. The rest of

67

the time we were in the town we didn't see her again, but every move into the streets or round a corner was accompanied by a wary eye open for a pretty blue and white dress. Never mind pickpockets, brigands, drunks, muggers... what we're worried about is a little girl in a blue and white dress.

It left a nasty taste. We should have said something, anything – "Listen, yes, we will give money to poor children who ask for it, but not if they behave like this..." Anything, to establish some contact, something to break through that quite monstrous and self-defeating act.

And yet she never stopped smiling. Through the whole thing, through all that onslaught and pursuit, there was a constant smile on her lips to the very end, and there was a proud calm in the smile somewhere behind the histrionics. For it was also a game, which she can hardly have expected to win, and quite possibly she went on her way when ejected from the hotel feeling that a small adventure of her devising had been accomplished, even an impersonal revenge achieved. I can't be sure of that, and perhaps she simply didn't know what to do.

She certainly had a great deal to learn about begging, but something completely different from begging was in possession of her. Her demand was for dues, as a right, with all the contempt. I guessed that this pride would either eventually get her out of her condition onto some eminence, or produce a complete disaster within four years.

b) LITTLE OLD CHILD LADY

A year and half later, in Sparti in Greece, we encountered her contrary. We were taking coffee in a donut bar on the main square, which seemed about the only place active enough to provide a view of local humanity. It was plastic and tiles, with some dozen consumers seated in its corridor-like space alongside the serving counter. A gypsy girl was begging round the tables. I think she was gypsy though she didn't have the physical features, but the headscarf, shawl and long skirt, all in gentle green and brown colours, suggested it. She was probably a small 14, and wore sandals on a cold day. What was startling was the elegance, the blown kiss. For she said little, and that quietly, and inclined her oval, charming, face and gently held out a cupped hand, not very far out, and got something, always, and then retreated with an animated smile and blew a kiss. Everyone, however little they gave, got the blown kiss – and graciously, with a little toss of the hand, tilt of the head and the warm smile. If it was acting it was good acting, there was no question of failing to respond to it. But it wasn't acting; it may have been a routine but it was meant.

After she'd done the rounds of the tables there was no dropping of a pose, no sudden hardness. The face remained calm, her movements smooth and gentle, she remained the little old child lady in the shawl as she sat at a table, counted her money and then went to order a sandwich from the counter. They knew her, and I'm sure she got some discount or something extra, probably without asking for it. She sat down again to eat, perfectly self-contained, not looking back at any of her benefactors, a task achieved.

I never saw anyone refuse a beggar in Greece, and the amounts they gave made us feel ashamed. We gave a few of the smallest coins and they gave notes. In a bar in Athens we saw two young working women in a bar give a small boy twenty euros each, without really being importuned at all. He just stood by their table holding a small accordion which he never seemed to use and they asked him about himself and got out their wallets. I wanted to call the little child-lady back and give her more, but she'd finished for now and quietly slipped out of the bar.

Is it a question of how to beg? or of virtue rewarded? Or a skill so finely tuned it can only derive from a quality of the heart? It wasn't demeaning and it wasn't insidious. What it meant was that she knew that the world was basically a good place, and what you just gave her proved it again. As for the future, you just prayed it would be kind.

The Walk to Poeinile Izei

We walk between two villages, Glod to Poienile Izei and back. We leave the car where the road ends in a stream hollow with wooden houses scattered round, and find the direction at a fork from a woman hanging out washing who speaks French and has, she says, spent several years in Paris. We have by now become accustomed to this constant easy helpfulness and unpredictability. To the fact that in a place where foreigners are almost never seen, a foreigner is not a surprise, nor a difficulty, nor an opportunity. Some people live here by choice. Strangers are sent to be helped

The track goes uphill and into open countryside, and thins to a footpath which meanders this way and that, up and down on undulating grassland thick with spring flowers. There are cultivation strips on all sides, with people working in them, usually a man and woman together. Man in shirt and thin-rimmed hat, woman in dark skirt, blouse and headscarf. They see us walking past and look up and smile and wave. And those close to the track stop working and look up at us, and say, "Hello. Where have you come from?" And we might say Glod, or we might say England, but usually we say England. "Oh", they say, "England. That's nice. Where are you going?" "Poienile." "Oh. That's not far. This way here." And they point. "Good-bye. *Drum bun* — good journey."

I think of walking in England, on the designated paths between the fields, where there might be an occasional person in a tractor, who might be friendly or not, if he could hear you anyway, or might be a servant of the master and narrow his eyes. Where it is very important who exactly is the owner, the entitled person with written proof, of the ground under your feet and whether permission has or has not been granted for members of the public to pass on that particular bit of the earth, and even if it's a useless bit of abandoned railway line the owner will still need to declare ownership rights by public notice and the employees will need to instruct, and remove, gently or not, those who transgress.

But here the ground between cultivated areas belongs to no one and is for the purpose of getting from one place to another, what does it matter who walks on it? What harm are they doing? I feel that I come from an irrational place.

The path tends to branch and multiply among the grassy hummocks, and may reconvene or not. Hardly more than a sheep track, it scatters itself across the spaces between farmed strips, its ramifications seem to be everywhere. There is a popular song all over Transylvania which says, "There are many paths across the fields; each one was made by a young man to get to his girl-friend's house." But every time we become confused or lost in this proliferation of paths, always someone pops up in a field holding a hoe. "Hello. Where have you come from?."… "Poienile? Oh, that's not far. This way over here…" At one point someone half way up a haystack fifty yards away notices that we are off the path and shouts over to us, "Poienile?" "Yes." "Left. Left." and sure enough there is the path, the little line in the long grass, five feet to the left of where we were standing.

Then over higher, rougher ground, and the path becomes again a track and starts descending towards the village visible below us. It falls quite steeply and curves into the village, a track shaped like a river: grassy banks on either side with paths on top of them and solidified mud in the middle, which in the autumn and late winter must be a liquid hell.

It seems quiet in the village. Beaten earthen roads, wooden houses. Things tend to fall into your hands in these places. We find the little wooden church, and wonder how to get in. A man leaning against a gate happens to have the church key in his pocket. Politely, always politely and willingly, he lets us in and shows us the famous Last Judgement wall paintings, rather demurely pointing out a demon with bellows pumping air into someone's arse as a punishment for farting in church. He leaves us and we sit in the graveyard, then go down to the village centre, get a couple of bottles of pop and sit on the wooden bench outside the bar. That's no problem, we know that now. We know that unless the village drunk happens to be about, no one will approach us or interfere with us in any way, indeed people will be so deferential as hardly to glance at us sideways, registering quickly that there are strangers in the village. The bar has a load of men in and about it as usual, playing cards and drinking. We sit and stare around, clouds gathering on one side of the sky.

There's a group of teenage girls, six of them, standing together outside the bar, wearing headscarves, white blouses and beautiful dark knee-length flower-patterned skirts. They know we're there but it doesn't disturb them. They talk together. We want to take a photograph of them they are so exquisite, but are worried about how they will react, go silly or flee in terror. The simplest way is to ask. "Can I take a photograph of you?" Of course you can, and they turn to face us and smile. They are not shy, or flattered, or proud, or nervous, they are slightly charmed. We take the snap, and remark on the attractiveness of their clothes. They look pleased, and close ranks again.

The return walk is threatened by massing cloud. The farmed strips are now unoccupied, but we find our way. On the quite lengthy trackway leading gently down into the village of Glod the rain starts in earnest. By the time we get to the car we are really very wet. But someone notices us, a woman standing in her gateway beckoning us over to her house to change our clothes…

Her house is sparse, wood, bare boards scrubbed pale. After the three-course meal, the brandy, the mineral water and the trying-on of the ceremonial jacket, we are led round the back of the farm to view the waterwheels of the fulling-mill. Crossing the plank bridge over the swollen torrent is a little worrying after the brandy. The sky clears. With very little language we are made to understand that the woman considers herself truly lucky that we landed on her doorstep in the rain. Strangers are sent to be helped. We drive on, down to the main road and up into the mountains that surround Maramureş, quitting this "peasant", this "backward" place, this, as they say in Bucureşti, "anachronism", to spend the night at the Borşa Ski Complex. There in the almost-empty concrete hotel we sit eating pork cutlets and chips while at the next table the restaurant staff and the local police abet the liaison between three young prostitutes and three businessmen. Welcome to the world of fitted carpets.

Sunday Evening in Botiza

A warm Sunday evening in Botiza after a scorching hot day, and of course many people are out in the streets and open spaces of the village. Lights on in the bar, and the food shop next door which is also a bar, and the hardware shop next to that, which is also a bar. Quite a lot of men sitting and standing outside the row of three shops, at tables or on the edge of the sidewalk talking animatedly with occasionally a murmur of song. Groups of men and women through the village, sitting on benches or walls or standing, some with bottles some not. Half a kilometre up the main street a big bar used by young people with music coming from it, crowded inside and spilling out into the street. People are not, as in some villages, very much dressed up for display on Sunday evening. They mostly seem to be as they would be any other warm evening, but more of them. Elderly people sitting on their verandas in narrow side streets, alone or in groups, speaking to each other and to passers-by. Nobody working: not washing clothes in the river, not carrying burdens or tools, not guiding animals. Children here and there, in groups or pairs, walking around, running, standing, talking, playing games. The young girls have the privilege of walking round in pairs in affectionate physical contact: arm in arm, arms over shoulders and round waists. People who meet kiss each other on either cheek. These things are coded. The priest's wife with her small dog on a lead, has crossed the big open space in front of the bars with the stream and bridge at the other side of it, and is standing talking to another woman, also in a dress and so probably also of the class designated "intellectuals" – teacher, doctor, etc. The dog sits obediently on the earth. There is a cart parked across from the bar with two horses waiting, occasionally rubbing their necks together. As the evening progresses light from the bars gradually seems to increase.

A six-wheeled heavy goods vehicle from the quarries or mines higher up the valley passes at a moderate speed along the main street, past the row of bars and on down the village towards the main road. It envelops everyone: men, women, old, young, children, babies, peasants, workers, gypsies, intellectuals, drinkers, loafers, talkers, singers, dogs, horses… in a thick cloud of grey dust.

The Funeral

I.

Popic said: You go to this place tomorrow, Valea Stejarului. You go to Vadu Izei cross the bridge and turn right. We just heard, there will be a death wedding. Iuga will be there with a video team. You go to my friend Popaşu who will look after you until it starts. Go early, arrive 11 o'clock.

We go. This place is not on the map. We cross the bridge over the Iza after Vadu Izei and turn right from the down-slope into a dirt area in front of houses, and this does indeed continue backwards as an unmetalled road, close by the river then turning slightly higher and into a small elongated side valley. It seems a long way, it takes a long time, the road is rough and there are some difficult slopes. There are always houses here and there, but by 11 o'clock the houses are continuous both sides of the road and we stop at a wider space where a wooden church is visible up the valley side.

It is unusually quiet. There are normally people all over the place in these villages, but this is like an English village not far from a town in the middle of a weekday. We fail to find Popaşu's house. We sit in the car and wait two hours. It's very hot and there's very little shade available. Occasionally a woman, always a woman, appears on the street, about some errand, and vanishes.

We wander up to the church, which is new, and notice in the graveyard the hole in the ground, ready for the coffin. We wander back to the car. This must be the right place, and it should be the right time, but nothing is happening and there's no one here. We wait another hour.

At 2 o'clock we get out of the car again and walk further up the village street, reaching an open space where there is a bar, closed, and a shop, closed. Outside the bar is a row of three seats and on one of them sits a man, a man between middle-aged and old. He beckons us over to sit down. The trouble is that the row consists of three chairs fastened together, like part of a cinema row, but the one in the middle has no seat, just the frame of one. I take this one out of courtesy and have to perch on the front edge of it, so that Beryl, who has the Romanian, converses with the old man behind my back as I swivel this way and that to acknowledge the two of them. Will there be a funeral here today? is the first thing. Yes, there will, if we wait. This man has a kind face.

And a serene temperament. He wears a checked shirt with pullover and the usual thin-rimmed hat. He has a long brown face with a large chin and a permanent resigned smile. He finds out what we are and registers no surprise beyond a minimal increase in the smile. He smokes, sits back, talks behind me from time to time. Yes, there will be a funeral, soon. And do you know, he says, this young man who has died, I will tell you how he died. He nods constantly as he speaks. This young man was 17 years old and he was with his friends on the mountain with the sheep. He got very hot running around after the sheep, and he drank very cold water from a spring. When he came home he was ill, he collapsed and was taken to the hospital, and on the third day he died. The doctors could do nothing for him. Now we must go down to the road near the church because the funeral will be here soon.

He is small and stooped but walks ably. The three of us go down to where the car is and sit on the benches of a house gate. There is no hurry, we sit in silence at first and then remarks are passed. He rolls cigarettes in newspaper. He digs a hand into his pocket and brings out a few coins which he shows us on his open palm. He is saying that this is his entire worldly wealth. He's not asking for anything, he is quite amused by the fact, he holds forth the coins with a big grin. They would not buy half a loaf of bread. A woman joins us, from one of the houses, bringing a plate of sweet cakes. We are told again the story of the boy who died.

Beryl runs to the car and brings back a small packet of coffee beans for each of them, which is one of the things you carry round with you in Romania to give to people. They are both quietly delighted. No one was anticipating a gift. The old man shakes his packet in his hand and smiles, as to say, I know good coffee, I shall relish this. Then he says look, the funeral is coming.

II.

Far away down the village street, which is fairly straight, is a blurred knot of people and some sound. It approaches, there is a drum beat, it stops and something takes place, and it approaches again. It reaches us as a crowd, a big crowd for such a small place, led by a cortège. Many people, young and old, walking together – not in procession but just all walking together – and at the front two grey horses pulling a cart decorated with carpets and textiles and flowers, the family of three sitting in a raised position at the front in black looking statuesque and devastated, and there is a wailing going on but it is impossible to know in the melée if it comes from them, whose faces are so closed. And behind them on the cart is the open coffin, feet forward, at its back the face of a young man staring with closed eyes into the sky. There is a little group at his head, of his age, one of whom, a young girl, holds a wedding crown in the air above his face. She must be the "bride".

Immediately behind the cart are three musicians: fiddle guitar and drum; they are playing wedding processionals. We can't hear this but we are told later. It all passes before us quite swiftly. The cortège stops in the wider space where the path to the church goes off beside the school. The coffin is closed, quickly, though at the last moment one of the men picks up a hat from the cart and pushes it onto the corpse's head – all the men in these places from maturity onwards wear thin-rimmed hats almost permanently and this was his. It is jammed affectionately and roughly on his head as a last farewell. Then the lid is set on and hammered home and the coffin is transferred to the shoulders of a team of young men, who bear it up to the church. Everyone follows it. Outside the church there is a halt, and the wailing stops on the instant while the priests take over. I get a feeling that funerals are common, that everybody knows exactly what to do and what comes next, that they have been here many times before, and it is all theirs; it hasn't been handed over to professionals who think it their duty to conceal from them the simple fact. After that the climax.

It reminds me of many things. Something which has been a long static preparation is now carried through swiftly to its conclusion. Like a sporting event which has hovered between one side and the other but at the end gives in to a sweeping victory. Like a protracted wedding ceremonial and feast towards the end of which the couple enter a vehicle and shoot off into the night. A long necessary slowness and a final liberating surge.

When the priests have finished the coffin is borne up again and carried into the sloping graveyard above the church, to the prepared hole in the ground. And with despatch – from now on there is no hanging around: every due has been paid and the rest is foresaid: get it over with. The lamenting remounts the moment the priests stop, and pursues the coffin up the hill. At the grave itself it is extraordinarily quick: no process here, no observance, this is the sign of the momentary act which ends and engenders everything. It is mainly aural. The wailing intensifies, the coffin is lowered into the hole, the ropes are withdrawn with a great roaring sound, and immediately thuds and thunder of soil and clods of clay being cast down onto the coffin by half a dozen men with long spades. I am convinced that these sound effects are purposeful, or that they are deliberately not avoided. The lad's mother passes from lamentation into open hysteria, shaking and howling, and is led away to be dosed with alcohol in a throng of voices...

And that's it, it's over. People hang around talking in small groups, and slowly everyone moves back down the hillside to the road. The mourners mount the cart and are carted off to pursue their eating and drinking at home. We meet up with Iuga who is in a state of excitement – "Did you hear? this is so rare now, they were playing wedding music… and do you know how he died? – Yes we have been told – It is amazing you know, that is exactly what they say around here will happen to you if you do that, and they say it will happen in three days. It would not kill me, and it would not kill you, but it killed him, and he didn't know, he was never told about this danger." Iuga is perplexed and animated by the mystery, as if on the edge of a different world. The crowd disperses into the village, and we are led to Popaşu's house, the woodcarver, a great patriarch who comes in laden with pitchforks from the fields and shows us his carving. He has an entire gateway laid out flat in his yard and we drink horincă as he shows us how he chisels at it. Iuga and Popaşu talk a lot and more horincă is drunk, then we move down to visit another woodcarver, a pupil of Popaşu. This woodcarver lives in a half-built new house, some of the rooms with breeze-block walls. He is engaged at present in creating a replica of a Napoleonic bed for a customer, a photograph from a magazine his only guide. There is much talking, we are given coffee, horincă and two hand-carved distaffs of extraordinarily complex geometrical design. And eventually, much later, we get to drive towards home, slowly down the track beside the river.

And where was our guide and help through all this, the old man with the fixed resigned smile who kept us happy waiting for the funeral? I remember when the crowd gathered below the church and surged up the slope he was there, encouraging us, saying without language: Come on, you don't want to miss this, keep abreast of the movement of the crowd to get to where it is taking place… don't be afraid, it's all right, and he swept us in front of him with a scoop of the arm. I glimpsed him once or twice after that, standing with the others, somewhat casually all of them, impassively witnessing the event. I thought he seemed a little saddened to lose us to Iuga. From the woodcarver's yard we saw him below, walking back with others up the village street, we waved and he signalled back. That was the last we saw of him.

When we sent a bundle of photographs back to Popic and Geta there was a good one of him in the cinema seat talking to Beryl, and we wondered if they'd know or recognise him and be able to pass the image on, probably not. I remember him best at the end of the waiting, sitting on a wooden bench shaking a packet of coffee beans close to his ear and winking at us – Yes, I know this stuff, I have known better times.

I remember this smiling face, of the poor man being kind to the rich. And I remember the grim unsmiling faces of the men on top of the soil-heap acting quickly to make all that noise as the clods hit the coffin and saying in it: No, we don't shield you from these facts, or this reverberation, it is kinder not to.

What it's all about

What it's all about, as far as I'm concerned, is that we have now been among these people three years running: our hosts, their relations, their neighbours, the relations' neighbours, the neighbour's relations, the people of Hoteni and the surrounding villages, people showing us the way, saying Hello to us in the fields, sheltering us from the rain, unlocking the church door, inviting us to their houses, giving us food and drink, showing us round... And among all these people, in this small zone of wooden villages operating a system of land tenure considered about a thousand years out of date where we come from, the attitude or response to us we have always met has been: How can we help these people? What can we do for them? How can we show them what they want to see, get them to where they want to go, feed them, brandy them, play music to them, give them of our produce, tell them what they want to know, guide them through the intricacies of our social customs, incorporate them into our households and families, and let them be happy to be here... and all without fuss, all in their stride, all getting on with their work to which looking after us instantly becomes integral. And even the little children in the village streets who call out to us as we pass, and men drunk at mid-day who stagger out of the village bar and buttonhole us, all they are really doing is seeking the opportunity to help us. Always calmly, always as a matter of course and custom: This is how we treat strangers here, this is the sort of place this is. And at no point is there the faintest hint of wanting anything in return, of any material kind, of anything beyond acceptance and appreciation.

So that it is a function of the structure, gladly enacted. There is almost no tourism here, so what we are remains "strangers" and as such we are no more than taking our rights, which are integral to the functioning of these places. There are no inns, hotels, guest houses, rooms to let, restaurants. Hospitality itself has for centuries serviced the necessary strangers, by whom it is possible to keep in touch with the world.

Back home, we have lost this. There might be reasons for thinking we live in a place which has gone wrong. There might also be reasons for thinking that people survive well enough through the most misleading structures. Or that the structure proceeds as it can't help proceeding here or anywhere and people generally make the most of it according to their resources. But as far as I'm concerned what it's all about is, that we have not retained this welcome to the other, implanted deep in the succession of persons, built into the language. Nothing remains meaningfully "built into the language" which is not maintained by constant use. We have lost it, and we live alone. I don't see any way out of this.

In one or two places (e.g. Săpinţa, Ieud) where tourism has made some ingress, it is not always the same. It can be the same, but we are sometimes approached in a way which is different, touched by a different need, which instead of "What can I do for these people?" asks rather, "What can I get from these people?" "What is there in this for me?" Something material is wanted back.

When I get back to Cambridge one of the first things I have to do is go to my bank, and there are a whole lot of notices and leaflets in it for their latest promotional campaign, which has the slogan, "Let us help you." There are posters and flyers all round the place in bright expensive colours with their headings confronting me on all sides: Let us help you – with your new baby / with your old house / with your car / with your marriage / with your business / with your holiday… I have been among "Let us help you" on the other side of Europe in places of the direst poverty for two weeks, and now I get the same message from one of the richest concerns in the world. I could be in a bank or I could be standing on a sloping dirt road in a village centre being approached by a drunken peasant who has opted out of an efficient self-sustaining system, and is constantly thinking one thing behind everything he says or does: "I want your money". "Give me your money".

Event at Deseşti

It is six o'clock on an October evening in Deseşti, the village below Hoteni on the river and the main road to Sighet. We have been sent here because there is, surprisingly, a "poetry festival" taking place. We have been promised twelve Romanian poets, which is rather more than we would normally have chosen to sit through, but we are assured that this will not be necessary; that part of it will be over. Already it is getting dark. There are lights on in the village hall and a few cars and about a dozen people standing outside it. We are waiting, we are told, for the poets to arrive. They were scheduled to be here at half past five. There are people in the hall busy preparing food, and children in the local costume running around here and there. Where are the poets? They are in the church, reading poetry and drinking. Would we like to join them? No, we'll wait till they've finished.

As always, people are terribly concerned to look after us and keep us informed. Drinking? That was what was apparently said. It will be the locally made fruit brandy, clear as water and said to be 60 percent proof, which accompanies all human intercourse in these parts. The poetry event happens here at this time every year because an important Romanian poet of an earlier generation was born in this village, and has a memorial room here, would you like to see it? It is a small room off the entrance corridor of the village hall, containing a display case on a table and some pictures on the wall, old photographs, letters, first editions. It has an air of disuse.

It is seven o'clock and the poets have not arrived yet, they are still reading (and drinking?) in the church. The church is a magnificent wooden structure of the 18th Century, the interior walls covered in a recently restored mural cycle. An occasional vehicle goes past on the road. We talk to the English teacher at the village school, who was a Russian teacher before the Revolution changed things. He explains the problems they have in the school, that there are not enough rooms and the children have to come in two shifts daily, and the classes are too large. But, he says, they get a good education, because they are extremely well behaved. They arrive as infants with "the perfect manners of the peasant" deeply ingrained. It is eight o'clock. Nobody shows the slightest signs of impatience. We have known this area for four years and we have never seen anybody show anything resembling impatience; I think it is an unknown emotion here. They stand around, talk, children in embroidered white costumes run among them now and then; if the apparent long-windedness of the poets is mentioned, it is with an indulgent smile.

At half past eight there is a stirring. They arrive. A small crowd, entirely male, comes down the rocky track from the church and crosses the road to reach the hall. What is it about poets, that you can recognise a bunch of them immediately on a dark road deep in the countryside? Is it the way they walk? They are obviously not locals, they have all the marks of the town-dweller, but neither do they move with the confident brusque solidarity of the businessman; they have rather a melancholy isolated look, a look of distrusting one's neighbour. They are very much a group of selves, with that "Where am I now?" look about them, as if they have been mobilised in some cultural cause for quite long enough and are getting bewildered. And the other question is, if they have been reciting in the church for at least two hours, to whom was this addressed? For there is no sign of any audience coming down the hill, just the dozen or so poets, plus a few poets' minders, two organisers, and the mayor.

We are set on five rows of chairs in the middle of the hall facing the stage, where the entertainment is to take place, provided by the local schoolchildren. But first the mayor, who is also the headmaster, gives an address of welcome. This goes on for a very long time, mainly because, as he himself explains, they have mislaid the fiddler who is to accompany the children singing and dancing, and the speech must continue until he is found. This is no problem. Whatever he is saying, the mayor is evidently eloquent and entertaining, and has already been very busy with the fruit brandy. The poets become comparatively animated and some indulge an exchange of repartee with the speaker. A brief biography of the mayor/headmaster is whispered to us: how he is a highly educated man who had a promising academic career ahead of him in philology, but chose instead to live in this small village because of his love of the place, and what a good manager he is in his dual role. He is certainly an expert impromptu speech-maker who has now been at it for 25 minutes, and the moment the fiddler turns up he rounds off and concludes his discourse in a matter of seconds.

The entertainment is exactly what we would have expected: circle dances on the stage, solo and group singing... a parody, in its way, of the social music and dancing it derives from, but nevertheless an utterly charming thing, sincerely offered, and accepted as far as I can see, gratefully by the assembled poets. And as often, there is one child of exceptional accomplishment, a girl of about 13 who sings some of the familiar local songs like a professional. It all goes on for a long time: it is normal to exercise the entire available repertoire on these occasions, and the locals invariably sit through these extended performances without the slightest lapse of attention or fidgeting, and it is greeted with warm applause when it ends. Then the dinner.

We were now in the hands of the principal organiser, a man we already know, a man of flamboyant and indefatigable presence who seats us opposite him and next to an elderly Romanian poet wearing the clothes of a town workman, who is obviously a dedicated exponent of the global grumpiness of poets. The local food is set before us (breads, cheeses, pork and cabbage leaf rolls) by women of the village, with plentiful amounts of beer and brandy, as our host, who has already put aside a considerable quantity of the firewater, speaks volubly in French about... well it is difficult in retrospect to say exactly what about, but there was plenty of it, with extravagant hand-gestures, and it embraced a great deal concerning the spirit of the place, and of poetry, and grandiose plans for next year's festival involving poets from many countries, since he has discovered that Maramureş "est en effet au centre de l'Europe." Dream accumulates upon dream in an ever augmenting flow of impassioned speech. A trio of professional musicians circulates among the trestle tables, the firewater flows, and whatever reason anyone is actually here for becomes increasingly a misty proposition. Anyone who passes within five metres of our corner of the table is ceremoniously introduced to us at length, beginning "I want you to meet an English poet...". This includes the mayor, now well over seven seas beyond but without any loss of polish, the other organiser, the talented girl singer (unbeatable for poise and charm) and half a dozen more. At one point I glance over our host's shoulder and see through an open door a small group of children outside, under the light of one of the street lamps, still in their costumes, singing and dancing in a small ring. It must be about midnight.

I have a vague recollection that we finally made our escape, in the middle of another profuse introduction, by performing a series of retreating dance-steps out through the door. The valley outside was settled into its normal vast and imperturbable night calm.

The Aunt at Breb

Then I noticed another woman, who came out of one of the outbuildings and walked across the yard and up the steps into the dwelling house. There are often other people – you think you've met the household and then you notice someone else, about some business or other, performing a useful task or helping to reduce the alcohol stocks or just belonging. But I looked again, because she walked strangely, her head turned somewhat sideways and upwards, her eyes directed over the rooftop, she walked briskly and without hesitation, but as if she didn't need her eyes.

She didn't, she was blind, and deaf. She was the aunt, and born like that: a congenital condition, for their mother, still living there though we hadn't yet seen her, was also blind, though not deaf.

These were the honey-makers. They had about a dozen hives in the garden and supplied the village. The constantly offered horincă was laced with honey, the bread was dipped in it, and when we left we took with us a former medicinal alcohol bottle full of the finest semi-liquid honey.

So the sister was born blind and deaf, and she was taken on, maintained, passed into the new household, permanently. There would have been no question about this, no asking "what to do about her". Everybody would have known exactly what to do about her. She sat with us later in the house as we dipped our bread in the honey, sipped the sweet brandy and prepared for the excursion to the pastures. She was small, looked about fifty, in the usual headscarf blouse jumper and skirt, a pale round face looking constantly pleased and yet as in a state of suspended question. She knew we were there, or something like us, something not usual. She sat on the bed edge with her head tilted and the family reassured her by touch from time to time, a single stroke down her arm with the flat of the hand in passing, to which she smiled in no particular direction. She wanted to touch us, to be sure we were there and who knows what other messages she might get from a hand on a hand, gently; then was satisfied with holding Beryl's bag.

Her intelligence, shorn of language, worked in the rhythms of her belonging, the flows and accessions of her participation in the ensemble of the household. It was a silent music, or an invisible text, constantly informing the inhabited spaces. I could read the text; it said, "This person is not a problem." But it said more than that. Her being was a whole book of this text.

When we were shown the buildings we entered the room she'd come out of, which was the weaving room, mainly containing the loom but also a bed, hers, against the wall. We think we were told that she could do some weaving by touch, though obviously she could not alone control the colour sequences. It was a light room of scrubbed wood, everything clean and of the highest quality. To wake up there in the winter, when the sun came in off the snow… And no light or sound to tell you you have woken up, just the resumption of being in the rhythms of touch and temperature, resumption of your expert knowledge of what you inhabit by its edges, and the people by their slightest acts of contact and proximity. It seemed obvious that here the text of this life, uninformed as to what people may be in the world, was able to locate its purpose.

We each touched her hand as we left, she was sitting near the door. That pleased her, obviously, and she knew then that the strangers were departing, and returned to her book.

Sunday Evening
in the Land of Oaş

At Baia Mare, I think Popic feels we deserve some real social music, since we'd hit a Lent-like post-Lent period in Maramureş when you're not supposed to sing or dance, so most of the music we got was at the children's festivals, and he proposes that we go to The Land of Oaş. They haven't been for eighteen months but it was always reliable, and it is Sunday evening.

The music played for dancing in Oaş is fiddle with zongora and drum, as in Maramureş, but the fiddle there is tuned up and reconstructed with shortened fingerboard to bear the extra tension, played with great virtuosity, very high and a lot of portamento, a kind of formalised screeching, while the zongora (an altered guitar) strums basic chords not quite at the junctures you'd expect, always pushing a high speed through the dance sequences. And there's a tight-throated forceful shouting-singing that goes with it. We know this music on record as something unique, but also as one of the most unaccountably ignored local musics of Europe. This is what we are going to find.

An hour and a half's drive, out of the town through a modern factory area and then quite a good main road along the edge of the Oaş Mountains – they come down towards you on the right, and the plain stretches away to the left. Through Negreşti-Oaş and on to Corteze where we turn off the main road. There is a distinct Sunday evening feel in these villages, quite a lot of people hanging around in no particular direction. Geta remarks disappointedly that no one is wearing the clothes of Oaş. One old man in a grey felt jacket with some white embroidery on it, the only one.

We reach the destination, the village of Bixad. Through the village centre, uphill on stones and dirt, over a hazardous bridge of concrete beams, down again, stop near the church, a modern one. This is the place. No one around, nothing happening. Just a village street, with a few half-wooden houses, sun beginning to get low. This is where the Sunday dancing takes place. Popic gets out of the car hoping to find something out and speaks to a passing man. His report back indicates that the man did not wish to be negative, in a manner of deference to the expectations of strangers which we now recognise: Yes, there could be a dance, here or a little higher up beyond the church, if you wait. Perhaps. If some people come, and the musicians also come, there will be a dance. We drive a little further and stop in a more open but very disused kind of space. Across the road is a modern brick building inscribed "Casă Culturului": the house of culture. It is so disused as to be close to dereliction, most of the windows broken, the ground around it full of heaps of stones. The declining sun shines through the windows from one side to the other. It is perfectly obvious that nothing is going to happen.

In a hope now somewhat forlorn, we take a different road back to stop at Bixad Spa, where there sometimes used to be Sunday dancing, but not so reliably as at Bixad. An open dirt space in the centre with a lot, indeed a crowd, of mostly young people in it, but not dancing: hanging round, hanging round. Chatting, holding plastic cups from a soft-drinks kiosk. And the spa, a "spring" under a wooden pavilion in a park-like space, actually a piece of black plastic hose-pipe emerging from the ground spouting water. Sharp, extremely salty.

So the Sunday dancing has stopped in the Land of Oaş too, as it has in Maramureş. Why has it stopped? Is it because of the economy? The men spend whole seasons abroad, out of this poverty-paralysed country, somewhere they can earn real wages for labour, and send it back home, return with it, have new houses built... Come back with their heads full of disco sounds? But there has always been migratory labour from all these terrains for centuries, right across the Austro-Hungarian Empire, and recruitment too, most of the village men normally working or fighting or being killed somewhere far away, and the dancing went on. The villagers have always known what goes on elsewhere, it never stopped them from dancing, indeed elsewhere is where half their dances come from. And it went on through Communism too, under duress, but it went on. And it stops, when? When local and kindred power structures begin to break up? When it is no longer needed as a preliminary mating ground because the young have plenty of other ways of getting together? I asked Lucy Castle why the dancing had stopped in Maramureş and she suggested it was something to do with a sense of shame, and of exclusion, as if it had become a provincial debility to know the old music and to dance to it. Not unconnected with media, and with media's promotion of a standardised village culture as a nostalgia market for the towns. So it finds itself on a shelf somewhere, not providing for itself but supplying a curiosity market to an absent public. Becoming part of somebody else's absurdity. Maybe. Something, anyway, more powerful than state directives and more powerful than war, has stopped the dancing. Why is it that deliverance from totalitarianism again and again takes on the aspect of long-term acquiescence to totalitarian aims? – the "rationalisation" of peasant culture, the village to end up as a commuter or geriatric dormitory with no generations, no trade, no custom, no dance.

Yet if the dancing were replaced by something that worked, whatever it was, some juke-box youth-bar society, some declaration that life promises more than an empty cup, there'd be no question of regret. But the dancing is replaced by hanging around wondering what to do on a Sunday evening in a small place with nothing to offer. The fiddler stays at home and does what, watches TV? Perhaps the fiddler was himself one of the men strolling around those village spaces as the sun got lower, chatting to the zongora player on a corner, their instruments hung up at home. And all those people, not just the old, they all know the dances, they all love dancing as anyone does, and singing, but they don't dance, and they don't sing.

Popic shrugs his shoulders. "Is all gone". Nobody knows why.

Driving back towards Baia Mare, the Oaş Mountains come sweeping down from the left and the great plain stretches away to the right. It is almost completely dark, and there are no lights anywhere except some scattered house windows. What are the social, political, developmental determinants of the silence in The Land of Oaş? What does it matter? If the result is silence, what is there to study? We might as well study ourselves. After all, we don't sing either; where I come from the great majority of people hardly ever sing, except, some of them, occasionally, in a specifically licensed and usually alienated structure. Why not? Because most people have been taught or received the notion, that they cannot sing "properly", do not have a "good voice"? At one time perhaps it was that, yes, but not now, now it's something else. I myself rarely sing, not right out. I don't sing because I don't know what to sing. I haven't got anything to sing which signals where I am. Oh, plenty to listen to, but no social music at all. Sometimes, back home, when I go walking alone in the hills I sing hymns as I walk; usually I make them up, with half-formed words. It seems the least offensive option. When I learned those cadences I was a novice member of a world articulating community. Now everybody dies alone.

We pass a nomadic gypsy wagon camped by the side of the road for the night. Not so much by the side of the road but half on it, and with no lights. We swerve slightly to avoid a ghostly canvas thing.

Efta Botoca

Left in charge of the house several rather chilly evenings in September, we moved to the front right or "music" room, the one which is not set out in decorative peasant magnificence, but is furnished for use. And I raided (with permission) Popic's store of recordings. I spent the first evening sampling: a big stock of mostly northern Transylvanian village or local music, which is not conceived as folklore, but simply as what it is called: musică populară, which means music of here, of the people, the only music actually made here and belonging here, whatever people listen to through loudspeakers. So, ordinary music, for social use, mainly for dancing, but also issued commercially on cassettes and available, sometimes, at small cassette stalls at the local markets, sometimes no more than a car with a cardboard box placed on its bonnet. A music right outside art/non-art categories, not because it transcends or pluralizes such categories but because it has nothing to do with them. And not out of ignorance – they know, Popic himself knows, plenty of classical, jazz, contemporary, whatever, music; they know it all exists, not as categories of music, but as music from other places, produced for other peoples.

Hundreds of cassettes stacked up horizontally on shelves in a corner of the room around the TV. Mostly fiddle music: at one end of the scale old Maramureş style with strummed zongora and drum, extending towards various modernised versions, Balkan or Turkish influenced, town-style or "gypsy" music, jerky syncopated version which they play in all the bars, and some downright beat versions. Also a few taragot players, who prefer big-group backing, but most of it lead fiddle with small group, and from all round the north and west: with zongora and drum locally, chordal viola and bass as it goes towards the west, or with viola / accordion band on the Banat, top end of the Great Plain, and further south. But the Oaş fiddlers not represented, who are so distinct in their soaring screeching displays, firmly localised, and, alas, on the way out. And near silence all round, outside the wooden house. The occasional dog bark, passing car or owl, nothing comes through the small dark windows.

The next evening I did some copying, and the only way to do that was to put my mini-disc recorder and mike on the table and take it from the speakers as I played the cassette, while we sat on the bench trying to be quiet. So the recording took in the whole ambience of the room and that didn't matter – the music stands out clear, against quite sharp cracks and creaks now and then of the floorboards and wooden surfaces as we creep about or manipulate cups and glasses of horincă. Also in the background the frequent bronchitic coughing of the old uncle, who's almost 90 and whose room is off the music room to the back – an alarming sound with its vocal attenuation of the initial eruption until you know that he's been doing this for decades whenever he lies down. And at one point the phone rings and the music proceeds while it's answered, and at another point the small round Unchi himself opens the door and appears on his way to the toilet in his alarming bright green night-shirt, and over the music the recorder faithfully records his extremely correct and archaic Romanian greeting as he passes though: "Good night to you most worthy dame and sir" or such-like. None of this matters; music lives on as ever through the interpolations of circumstance.

I copied the work of two musicians. First, Mihai Covaci, known as "Diavolul", the Devil, virtuoso fiddler from Vadu Isei with only three fingers on his left hand because of an agricultural accident, after which he re-taught himself to finger. Straight and particular Maramureş fiddling in the old way with zongora and drum, a mass of trills and ornamental figures through which the known dances stand like statues: învârtita, joc, horea… and the slower numbers for listening, or rather as they prefer around here, for drinking, "de băut". His only issued cassette I think, some years ago, you never see it in the markets now. Also an unissued recording on cassette of Diavolul playing with Popic himself on zongora and singing; technically a disaster, with hiss, flutter, drop-out and everything else, but the performance comes through, the full flight of it.

Which was wonderful, and all I needed. But there was another one which, in sampling, I kept going back to, a fiddler I'd never heard of, again doing Transylvanian melodies but differently, without any of the local insistence, the grounded edge. No digging in, no native entrenchment but a quite pure version, even ethereal. Efta Botoca, it said, with the usual picture of someone in a straw hat playing a violin. Issued by Electrecord, STC00661, no date, recorded in Satu Mare but coming, I think, from further south. No other credits except George Vancu, "Orchestră", which means accompaniment and in this case, which was one of the startling things, sounded like no more than a single chordal viola under the fiddle plus sometimes a string bass, supplying the harmonic and rhythmic rationale of the music with the same rather detached professionalism, and on only five tracks a bigger ensemble. Dance pieces as usual, with some slow songs, doine, given out so calmly, with all the usual restless ornamentation expertly delivered but in this case restful. I couldn't easily think of anyone dancing to this music, but rather remembering dancing, it had that bitter-sweet distance, though I knew that he must have learned his trade on the dance floor and in a different situation, with a different band, could obviously sustain a wedding or any such demand. And there was in the playing a sense of freshness and enrichment, and tremendous assurance. It was one of those works which solves something, and the performer knows it.

"Efta Botoca!" Popic said several days later, "you found him!" and laughed. "He was one of the first, who gave us the idea." By which I think he meant, to get rid of the drone, restore the chordal middle, extend the harmonic vocabulary, let the contours of the piece emerge. But also the "orchestră" reduced to just one or two players, delicately underlining turns of the melody with enriching modulations and returns. After all the Communist era massification of this music, to return not to standard practice, but to a newly coined simplicity, and an acknowledgement, that you are not in the same place. "He's dead now. That's the only cassette he made."

And there I was, somewhere up in the distant hills, seeking to prove that virtue operative locally is the necessary predicate of global hope, that a small-scale structure holding people to their inherent, pre-natal, promises, was a model of the post-nation diplomacy the world is going to need if it doesn't sunder into large-scale violence. And I found Efta Botoca.

Who, however far away in whatever niche of the Carpathians, is remembered. Two weeks later, at the great annual market at Feketetó on the Cluj-Oradea main road I asked after him at a cassette stall. It's a Hungarian market, and the Romanian music on sale was mostly the trumpet-violin of the middle Banat, and they hadn't got him. But the man smiled and said, "Da," (yes) "Efta Botoca", and nodded his head dreamily as if reminded of something quite close to the heart.

Efta Botoca. It's a name which, if you mention it to people, either it means nothing to them whatsoever, or they immediately smile. So there is an aperture of hope.

Quiet Pastures
with a Small Thunderstorm

Paths fan out and disperse from each access point: tracks running between houses in the village, over bridges, between orchards and then spreading out into the open pastures. Tough grassland with thinly scattered trees and bushes, many of them small apple trees – dark red apples in season, small hard and sweet, now sparse white blossom. But also plum, nut bushes, clustered or isolated, a lot of small birches. Small rough fields occasionally impinging on the edges of the pasture, in different places every year. And haystacks, of which these are last year's, dark brown, beehive-domes, built up round a slender central wooden post or trunk, on a stone base. The pastures slope gently down towards the river.

The pastures slope down towards the river. Very quiet, distant rattle and slush of the river, faint groan of a vehicle on the main road beyond every ten minutes or so. A distant shout or dog bark from one of the villages. Very few birds around, just an occasional dart and twitter, minimal signs of any other creature, such as rabbits, scattered crickets chirping. The land is in use, open unfenced untracked land disappearing into the distance devoted entirely to its purpose, shaped by it, face to face with the village, there is really no room for wildness. Hoteni's animals will be out here somewhere, with their herdsmen. The beasts are led home every evening at six past Popic's gate, at the last count 25 horses, 7 cows and 42 buffalo – the Indian kind, bos bubalos, water buffalo, with heads like shovels. And sweet bright white milk. That is who these pastures belong to. They are in the keeping of the commune of Hoteni for 25 horses 7 cows and 42 buffalo. It is their land.

It is all theirs. We pass a herdsmen's shelter, an open room, thin roof with four posts holding it aloft, plastic bags of buffalo milk hung up to curdle for cheese. And, normally, a few of those big cuddly killer-sheepdogs hanging around or sleeping, but deserted this afternoon. And possibly sometimes, the tilinca, shepherd's flute, to pass the time, maybe still, well, I never yet heard a transistor radio out here. Far in the distance the *tok tok tok* of the water-mill at Hărnicești, upstream, and a faint roll of thunder.

A faint roll of thunder and some drops in the air, but nothing to stop for. It increases somewhat and we crouch close together in a clump of bushes as it patters round us, then it lessens and we walk on. Above the pastures the landscape is hill and forest on all sides, this whole arena is ringed by hills, low hills with forest. A small thunderstorm, marked visually by a knot of fire-red and indigo-blue cloud, travels round this circumference from south to north-west. It rumbles and it sheds rain but it doesn't advance towards us, it keeps to the horizon. The air currents are circulating round this zone of open protection like a holding arm. They push a small thunderstorm clockwise.

These People

"…You go there, and these people, they can't do enough for you. They help you with everything you could possibly want. They invite you into their homes, feed you, brandy you, lodge you, for weeks at a time. They show you whatever you want to see, they arrange for friends or relatives to host and guide you when you travel to other villages. If you want music they fix up music for you. They lend you any clothing you need for the weather. If your car breaks down they get it mended for you, and nobody wants paying for it. You have to fight to get them to accept money for anything. When it's clear that you are attached to the place on a long-term basis they even offer to arrange a house for you there, if you want, a wooden house in the fields for the rest of your life for the price, in U.K., of a garden shed. When you leave they give you food for the journey and a litre and a half of the local brandy, and they sniff and get weepy, because you're going."

We wander around Vişeu lost, looking for the office of the mountain railway. We ask a young couple who are walking across one of the squares, students or scholars on their way home. Yes, they say, we can help you. They are with us for two hours. They take us to one office, where they inquire on our behalf, then three kilometres to another, outside the town in the wood yard which the railway serves. They interpret the notifications for us. They discuss the timetable and prospects with various persons who are hanging around the place and report back to us. They hitch us a lift back to town in a lorry, and lead us to the best place for a quick afternoon drink. Then they accept a lift to their house down the valley where they entertain us with tea, cake, brandy, until reluctantly they accede to our departure. They live in a small house in a kind of Palmerean dell with a stream flowing through it, down off the main road through the village.

"And then these people, like for instance, that young man from Vişeu, they set out travelling, because they need well-paid work, something has happened, say, the father is in hospital and they need to earn money for the family for a year or two. They float with minor obstruction across Romania, though Hungary, Austria, Germany, Belgium and France, and they reach Calais. They then seek to cross the Channel, and enter Britain, and they are treated as vermin. They are treated like contaminated meat."

Ana

A new notice appeared in Hoteni village, inviting visitors to walk to the "lake", and pointing up the Breb road, with a map. There were botanical and geological notes, and it was claimed that turtles lived there. We were returning from a walk, four of us, with time in hand, so we took the option.

You go up the Breb road and where the houses start to thin out take a little-used track to the left, a sunken track with a lot of vegetation and mud in it, about 2 kilometres to the top of a slope. Then there is a dip, or cleft of ground, but no water to be seen, only a dense clump of low dark bushes occupying the bottom of the hollow. Doubtful if this was truly the "lake", we sniffed around the edges. The ground under the bushes was black and looked damp, that was the nearest to a lake available. The bushes, whatever kind they were, were impenetrable and we peered under them not dreaming for a second that we would suddenly spot a turtle.

After sending one of us to the top of the bank in case there was a real lake beyond, we started back down and the rain began, suddenly and heavily. By the time we were near the bottom of the track we were unhappy even in our waterproof clothing, and turned off the track towards a house visible through the trees for shelter. You can always do that and you'll be welcomed, though there are risks involved. It was the usual kind of house, quite old, small as they go, with a new house being built in front of it, entirely of wood, with three men working on it. We were invited into the unfinished house and were told that unlike most of the villagers they preferred their new house to be made of wood, because they thought it made a better house. This seemed encouraging. After a few minutes we were transferred to a small summer kitchen in an outbuilding, sat round a table, and the young wife was in charge of us. Her name was Ana.

The kitchen was a dark hole with a curtain as a door. The rain beat upon the metal roof and dripped through it in several places. Ana was short and energetic, with waved black hair, and leather jacket. She bustled around the blackened stove producing coffee and, of course, poured out four substantial glasses of brandy. None of this happened very quickly, because Ana also talked. She had been working for two or three years, on and off, as a servant in Paris and acquired enough French to hold forth in it, and did, though as she got more and more involved in what she was saying she increasingly slipped into Romanian. We sat, and she stood before us and talked: the old house, the new house, her upbringing in Hoteni – she was a childhood friend of Geta, whose parents were their closest neighbours down the hill. The family, the husband. What a terrible state Maramureş is in. "The agriculture here is a disaster." Terrible poverty and toil everywhere. Can't wait for EU entry to come and save us. We need foreign money. We want to see all these little smallholdings become big mechanised farms. Paris paid for the new house. How they make you work there, how rich they are. Her first employers were Jews and they were very unkind, and had too much money. Terrible people, but Jews are like that. All Jews are very rich and unkind. All these things at length and quite forcefully.

Ana didn't stop. Neither, unfortunately, did the rain, still pounding the roof, so it was difficult to propose a departure, or to find a gap in which to propose it. A second round of coffee and brandy. Occasional interjections from us were not taken very seriously: "Not all Jews are like that you know" – this just set off a repetition of the diatribe against Jews who are all rich and bad people; "We like Maramureş very much" produced a repetition of its disasters. After we had been there at least an hour the rain slackened somewhat, and we left slowly amid profuse thanks, hailed farewells to the house builders, and slopped on down the muddy track.

Sometimes you wonder if you've got it all wrong, and this place really should, for the sake of its inhabitants, be closed down. For that's what it would be, maybe will be. Industrial farms and tourist centres. They who successfully resisted collectivisation during 50 years of Communist and sub-Communist rule, now to volunteer themselves into it for what they see as the easeful life, and abandon independence. The village changing from an association of smallholdings to a landowner's property. Most of the historians and commentators I trust (Mak, Gellner, Judt...) have a dislike for rurality. Judt, driving through Transylvania, sees the horse transport and the strip fields as a sign of Romania's post-Communist failure, as much as the urban slums and the industrial wreckage. Perhaps a few hours at Popic's place will restore our faith, especially as Diavolul is coming to play this evening. Perhaps the performance, and the purpose of the whole enterprise, will re-convince us of the falsity of the either/ or options. And that whatever gets imposed there will be a resistance to it which is not necessarily retrograde, but a different modernity which opens a future to the world, and can be heard in the air.

But Ana has seen the turtles, several times, when she was young. The children would go up there when there was a lot of water around and they'd see the turtles in a group. She was frightened of them.

Goodbye for Another Year

In the evening we go over to the parents' farm, to say goodbye. After the cake and horincă in the summer kitchen we find ourselves, as you so easily and surprisingly do, wandering freely and unaccompanied around the establishment, walking through the kitchen garden, leaning over the pig sty... It's a warm evening, the sun now getting quite low and its light deepening and seeming to settle on the wooden buildings among the orchard trees, "bathing" them, getting under the porch roof, "peering" as a poet might once have said, or "descending like a benediction" and why not? Why not say such words, in a place like this?

The big old Mama is busy with her preparations, the little old Papa has disappeared again into one of the sheds to attend to something. Voichiţa, the unmarried daughter, is sitting sewing in the front porch, the sunlight "peering" at her from the side. She is in a framework of carved wooden posts and beams. Beryl leans on the rail and talks to her, in English because Voichiţa needs practice in it, she wants to become a teacher, though it will be very difficult to get the qualification and land a job, especially around here, where she wants to stay. She wears a white and blue cloth wrapped round her hair, and bends over her work, smiling and speaking softly.

In front of the porch is a pot-tree. That is, a small tree stem stripped of bark, its branches trimmed to a foot or so, with a collection of pots and pans hung on it, inverted over the branch stubs. At one time this would have been Voichiţa's tree – these pot-trees are meant as a sign to the passer-by that there is a marriageable daughter in the house. Voichiţa has always been a prime exemplar round here, in her youth, of someone who can bear all the serenity and dignity of a "peasant" family into a modern elegance, the calm of continuity and the sparkle of sophistication. The idea of her being on offer via a pot-tree is absurd. But it's there, as, I suppose, a gesture of belonging, emblem of solidarity, one of the devices by which a glow of native certainty descends on the house. It puts you in a landscape.

Before we go we say to her, "We shall be coming again next year. What is there we could bring with us, what can you best use that you can't get here?" And she looks at us, as at two nice children who don't quite get the picture, and says in a perfect English which is rare for her, "Really, there is nothing we need. There is nothing at all." And she means it.

Over the Border

When you cross from the north-east of Hungary into Romania, you remain in the same terrain. There is no geographical feature to mark the border, as indeed why should there be since it was a purely political creation. The great plain continues, completely flat and farmed on a large scale, great extents of green either side of the road with hardly any buildings in sight and nobody around.

There are two major border towns, Oradea and Satu Mare, both of which at the 1919 division fell to Romania and so are now dilapidated and impoverished. Oradea is a Hungarian merchants' town full of extravagant secessionist piles, yellow green and pink art-nouveau monstrosities on all sides with fantasy turrets and pinnacles, curvilinear ironwork balconies and doorways, scrolled window-surrounds – all soiled, peeling and semi-vacant, all the restaurants no more than bars, all the shops short-stocked. In the evening you stroll the old town in streets of one-storey houses, and through the windows see dim light-bulbs illuminating bare living spaces. And of course there are beggars, in Satu Mare many of them, mostly children. The small Hungarian towns close to the border on the other side mostly seem sad places, neglected and dull, but there is no sense of this plunge into poverty.

But the countryside looks almost the same, great unbroken stretches of level green, until you start noticing, increasingly, as you progress into the country, marks of poverty. In the towns the marks of poverty mean distress and failure; we're used to them, but they are depressing. In the countryside we notice the marks of poverty as delightful and welcome things. The first sign that we have truly arrived is the first horse-drawn cart we see, of which we shall see hundreds before we arrive anywhere, always with a red tassel hung on the left side of the horse's head, slowly trundling along in and between villages with their necessary loads. They are signs of poverty, like the bad road surfaces, the unfinished new buildings everywhere, the endless successions of old low rural houses in their orchard yards, the lack of traffic, the people on foot... The further you get from the border the more people there are on the land, working small strips or watching sheep, and the more there are walking on the roads, and these too are signs of poverty. In Hungary nobody around, an occasional tractor in the fields. And we delight in the signs of poverty, as if we have arrived in some flourishing place. Do the Romanians hate this poverty? Do they hate their horses?

When we first went to Ireland, in 1973, every morning, wherever you went, you would see little one-donkey carts, each with one person idly floating a whip in front of him or her, each bearing one churn of milk to the dairy in the nearest town. They moved slowly, the drivers looking around them as they trotted on, saluting people they passed, familiar or strangers. Ten years later they had all vanished. The milk got to its depots from big farms by tanker. There was no one on the roads but the cars and the lorries and the tankers. Did the Irish hate their donkeys? Did they loathe and detest the gentle obedient creatures, their marks of poverty? When they got back to the smallholding did they kick their donkeys for being indexes of low economic status?

Indeed they did not. But they got rid of them. And entered the "Irish economic miracle." But are the highest house and food prices in Europe the kind of "economic miracle" that serves us best?

Every year we enter Romania from Hungary by car, and shall continue to as long as we are able, and we shall watch the roads as we enter the country, and notice what is moving on them. They might keep the horses. It is a remote chance, it depends on dumping thirty years of redundant heavy industrialisation and moving forward into a more delicate future, in which the capital power is reduced to an obedient functionary and people accept to live as almost all the rest of the world lives, in a thriving and toilsome poverty, possibly consoled by a slow dawn of access to micro-electronic speed and scope. So you drop your shame and resignation without sacrificing your pride – nobody is entitled to make you feel backward; you are behind the "modern world" because you are ahead of it. I wonder if this could happen, here or anywhere. As if a choice were made between poverty and affluence which was recognised as a choice between labour and ease, and then as between purpose and emptiness, and then as between hope and despair…. and people opted to remain within the terms of life.

These are crazy notions I have, of course, I know these are crazy notions. But I wonder if it might in fact happen, and we'd get here, you and I, somehow, twenty-five years hence, in our late seventies, and notice as we entered the country the horses still on the roads, carting things around in return for their keep, plodding along getting in the way of the few cars and lorries, blocking the road in the village centres where people want to stop and talk. Signs of poverty, signs of pride, signs of knowledge. Small, strong, dark brown horses with red tassels hanging on the left sides of their heads.

The Room at Lunca Ilvei

Bistriţa-Nasăud region, on the inner edge of the great mountain and forest barrier that runs down the eastern side of Transylvania, and gave it its name. A village thrust up into the edge of the forest among the foothills, on a platform at the top of a long valley, all its meadows folded into dramatic hill-slopes and shoulders among forest outcrops. A long thin village heading towards the forest edge, at the far end of which the Englishman keeps his establishment, a stable of 20 horses and touristic facilities. We arrive unexpectedly and there are already four English on holiday in the village – close to capacity. Accommodation is found for us in a village house a little further up the road, next-door-but-one to several large heaps of timber.

We are shown into the room by the woman, who as usual is in sole charge of us. But this is not the usual woman; in the rural smallholdings the woman in charge is usually a senior figure, even a grandmother. This is a much younger woman, with one child of about four, a charming presence, wanting only to please, covered in smiles, always stooping slightly and clasping her hands together under her chin to ask and show us. The husband is a carpenter, he makes window-frames, we don't see him, and there is at least one more man in the house. She obviously does all the domestic work, cooking, and child care, and we hear noisy complaints in the evenings, but she attends us with assiduous duty and giggly charm.

The delights of staying at this establishment. 1. Nobody speaks English or French. 2. There is a bench outside you can sit on, facing south towards the bulk of the village which you can't see, but you can watch what passes on the road, people on foot and the occasional horse and cart, and the layers of blue wood-smoke floating over the roofs in the early evening. 3. The evenings are getting quite cold and the room has a tiled wood stove. On the first evening she shows us how you get the fire going well, then completely shut both the bottom air-vent and a trapdoor in the flue above the stove. The burning wood then goes into a catatonic suspension and gives off liberal heat for eight hours without consuming itself away. At eight in the morning the tiles are still hot. 4. We are brought breakfast and dinner in our room, and we eat what they eat when they can afford it, which is now, because of us. 5. At the end, asked how much we should pay her, she has absolutely no idea, and just hunches, and bares her palms, and smiles.

But the room. In fact there are two rooms, front and back, the back for sleeping. They are both small and, the back especially, crowded out. But not traditionally, this isn't "peasant" décor – no antiques dealer even from somewhere as desperate as England would look twice at any of it. What is traditional is the crowding itself. Anything not from the shops of the nearest town is from a souvenir-stall somewhere, but above all there is a mass of it. Disneyesque ducks on the wall in a factory-woven fabric of repoussée nylon. Bright acrid multicoloured floral cloths draped everywhere. Walls crowded with reproductions, photographs, prints. A glass cabinet full to bursting with unused fancy glass and ceramics, Christian dolls, souvenir products, none of them from very far away. A model cathedral. A small Virgin shrine above our bed-head with blue battery-operated lights which never go out, at night in the warm black mug the only way of tracing verticality unless a thin line of red glow escapes from the edge of the stove's door. An arc of five tiny blue stars floating in the black warmth.

So that the things you store and treasure against time don't refer you to where you are and what you know, but, even at this proximity to the forest, to their precise opposites.

The BBC at Lunca Ilvei

A BBC camera team with a well-known presenter had been sent to Transylvania to make a programme to be shown on Hallowe'en, with emphasis on the creepy: ghosts, vampires, wolves, etc. Why else should they come? What else could possibly interest anyone about Transylvania? They turned up at Lunca Ilvei and were housed in some kind of hostel down the village, the four of them. They knew what they wanted.

They wanted a night campfire meeting, immediately. They had no spare time, it must be tonight. It was arranged, in the fields behind the stables. A quite large bonfire was got together during the afternoon and word went round to about twenty villagers and us. The two village musicians were also needed – accordion and fiddle. These were smallholders who played locally as a hobby or for slight extra income, and their repertoire was a selection of pieces from all over the country. The accordionist was quite good, though his forte was small flutes; the fiddler was rather ineffective, but the accordion carried most of the music.

As it got dark the fire was lit and the cast was assembled on a grassy bank in front of it, sitting on the ground or standing, in a small arc, which by careful camera control could be held to represent a whole circle of rustics around the fire. The ground was damp and quite muddy, and a strip of plastic had been put there for sitting on, hopefully not evident on screen. In the centre of the arc sat the presenter, an Irishman, interviewing Julian, illuminated by the glow of the fire. The BBC had supplied two crates of beer for the crowd, which were appreciated, and mainly because of this, I think, the general atmosphere was happy, in spite of the artificiality of the situation and the discomforts involved.

Because unless you got into the direct shine of the fire it was rather cold and there was an occasional slight swirl of rainfall. Also sitting on the plastic on the ground was not too easy and there was a tendency to slide slowly downhill. But still the general atmosphere was happy; people chatted, drank the beer from the bottles, and the musicians played, with some people singing among themselves to some of the tunes, and the interview proceeded.

Julian is a good raconteur. Stories about bears and wolves. About finding a bear up your apple-tree in the morning. How wolves would come down to the village from the mountains in the winter and he'd sometimes hear the howling at night. The presenter was obviously not very bright and things went best when Julian himself led the talk on from one thing to another, under the presiding spirit of the zuică he was consuming. There was also interplay with the villagers, jokes aside in Romanian which might have said anything for what the BBC knew but which the company thought were very funny. In particular there was among us an adolescent girl, a member of Julian's casual house staff, who was apparently very sensitive on the subject of "boys", to whom Julian would throw suggestive remarks which got squealing responses from her and the whole thing went down very well with the crowd.

The trouble was, whatever was said and done, the presenter or the producer immediately said, "Do/say that again", including all the casual banter in Romanian. Everything had to be repeated, a second or third time for a better camera angle or sound take. Of course it was never as good the second time, and very much less entertaining for the villagers, and these doublings made the whole thing drag on. And there were other troubles, such as inane questions which Julian had to cope with, and try to make the chat interesting again. And the cameraman had his own problems. He was evidently very good at his job, working dextrously with a hand-held camera, but had been eating unwisely since he entered the country and was suffering from a fairly severe attack of "the shits". So the proceedings were interrupted again and again by him handing his camera to the nearest BBC-person ("Hold this a minute will you") and dashing off into the darkness, directed loudly by Julian to a group of trees at the back of the field.

It took quite a long time. Finally the BBC crew looked at each other and said, "That's it, we've got enough." They got themselves together, and moved out, escorted back to their waiting car and driver, quite thankfully I think because the cameraman wasn't the only one who was ill and they all looked tired, and they had to get up next morning for a horse-and-trap ride through the forest to Castle Dracula, a renamed 1980s ski hotel about 20 kilometres away.

But the musicians played on, and everyone stayed. And they did some very popular numbers which most people joined in on, and the dancing started. It was colder and darker and there was fairly definite gentle rain, which nobody paid any attention to. The fire was a big heap of glowing embers now and in front of it they danced in the mud, for about an hour. Twirling, elegant, couple dances, in mud. It was the best part of the evening, by a long way.

The Dance at Mociu

Jehovah's Witnesses are there, distributing free packets of soap with attached tracts. They never miss a chance, in a zone where a bit of free soap really makes a difference. But when you enrol you hang the fiddle on the wall for ever.

A grassy slope with small trees leading up to the village hall or "House of Culture", with people all over it waiting, sitting on the grass, standing talking in groups. A beer stall opens, its cooling device a bucket of water. We buy beers for the band from Soporu, most of whom we brought here – usual directives: "Yes there will be a dance at Mociu on Sunday afternoon; perhaps you wouldn't mind giving the band a lift there." There is a small man in white shirt black trousers and waistcoat flat out on the ground snoring. "This is the bass player. He is very tired, he was playing for a wedding all night." We have tried our best to disillusion them, but I think Şandorică's family still think we are something important, impresarios or agents or record producers, something from which future benefit may result. Wishful thinking, out of near desperation: "Nobody wants this music any more".

We sit on the grass with the band's family, communicating with and through the son-in-law, called George though at the time we thought it was Ivan, in about one percent of the German language. And suddenly, whether in connection with misapprehension of our status, a thank you for the beers, or a pure gesture of welcome, Şandorică comes over to us with the viola player and a bassist borrowed from the Mociu band, theirs being still prostrate, and they stand in front of us and play a slow dance number specially for us. From that point we have arrived, and the whole trajectory has been worthwhile. The days of travel, the empty concrete hotels, finding the village, asking at the bar/shop, getting involved with the village drunk, finding the house, struggling with the language, all that kind of thing, it had got us somewhere.

Our first sight of the band leader and two of his subordinates three days earlier, standing outside the bar in Berchieşu wearing straw hats and each holding a hoe, vertically, like a spear. "Look at this, this is no condition to find musicians in, look at their hands…" George, who brought us there in our car from their home in Soporul, said something like this in something like German. And they insisted on buying us lemonades, and said there would be a dance in Mociu next Sunday, "Perhaps you wouldn't mind…"

And how you can't enter a Transylvanian house without being treated as a guest should be, supplied with food whatever time of day it is, and coffee or alcohol, and generally treated to utter welcome, comprehending or not. I think it was on our first visit at their house, through George's German (if George was indeed his name) that the misapprehension about our being a film-crew began. On our second visit, the morning of the dance (more cabbage rolls, more coffee…) they were evidently troubled because to make video films in Romania you have to have a government permit and we might not have one, and we also didn't seem to have a camera. "You have a video camera?" asked Şandorică, in no language that I specifically remember. "No," I answered similarly, "we have ears" and flapped one of mine with a finger. He laughed and I think the misapprehension began to crumble from that point on, and our entire insignificance as it dawned on them seemed to do nothing but increase the welcome.

They said they weren't gypsies but they lived in the gypsy street of Soporul. And when we left them that first time, taxiing the car very slowly down the stony road between wooden fences towards the open spaces of the village centre, each house as we passed it suddenly produced "gypsy music" from their cassette-players turned up to full volume, quickly reverting to global corporate pop after we had passed.

Two hours late we are ushered in, conducted to seats, and the dance starts. Village Sunday dancing has stopped everywhere in Transylvania, and this one has been organised by a government-supported cultural association from Baia Mare. It is not in the open air where a Sunday dance always was, it is being recorded, and two troupes of young folklorical formation dancers from Cluj and somewhere else have been invited to take part. There are three officials in charge and a man from Germany quietly recording everything, and Jehovah's Witnesses have given out their soap packets. But it is still the real thing. You know this as soon as Şandorica's bow touches the string. There is no question of it. The social necessity may fade and crumble, but the music maintains its force, because the force is upheld by a beauty. For how much longer?

While the response is still there. Dance after dance, the Soporul band driving its music relentlessly through the event, alternating with the band from Mociu itself, more of a gypsy band, dark and concentrated, the leader playing a left-handed violin. An opening promenade and then long suites of elegant couple dances, with sections of male display dancing: solo, right in front of the musicians and in constant eye-contact with the leader, leaping and calf-slapping. These people may have discontinued the Sunday dancing, the mating structure it represents being after all entirely superseded, but they have not forgotten how to dance. The men in basic local dress with beautiful embroidered coloured belts, the women in ornamented white dresses – but not necessarily, for it is not only the older people who take part. The elegant daughters, for instance, of Şandorică, and several others male and female, in completely urban dress, one of the girls even wearing trousers, are there in the midst, secure in every step of the old dances.

It isn't a Sunday village dance, but it's Sunday and the village dances, which is the main point. The musicians in fact feature rather more than the dancers – it is they who are on show now, the cameras and the microphones focused on them, but Şandorică leans forwards towards the old gent in the felt hat stepping and leaping in front of him, and eye into eye they create the occasion together.

And the peasant-uniformed formation teams from the towns over the hills get their turn, the appropriate music produced by the band somewhat stiffly as they follow their routines. They are young, and the regarding villagers indulgently commend them. And as communal dancing resumes suddenly a young man with an alto saxophone has joined in, with high-speed virtuosity and perfectly in accord except that his instrument is too loud, and pushes the stringed instruments into a corner.

And then, after one of the fast dances from the Soporul band has got under way, most people instead of dancing are gathering round one couple and watching them. A gypsy lad of about sixteen and his mother are dancing together to the music, quite differently, either as an intuitive response to the music or in a version gypsies have developed at home for their own entertainment, for gypsies would never traditionally have been allowed to take part in village dances, in fact in most villages it would have been regarded as an appalling violation of propriety. But they do now. They step and prance rhythmically, facing each other, with a lot of fast hand leg and foot movements, and it is a quite virtuosic performance greatly removed from the elegant twirling and side-stepping of the formal inherited version. The villagers just gather round and admire, forming a crowded circle with a small central space in which the gypsies dance. There doesn't seem to be any sense of critique, that the gypsies might be doing it "wrongly". They are admired for their resourcefulness and verve. And they are gypsies too, and that only seems to enhance the admiration, as if people for so long excluded and despised gain the right to participate in their own terms.

So it seems in the festive space. The Jehovah's Witnesses departed long before the dancing began. The poverty they exploit resurfaces when the dancing stops. In the post-event bustle the viola player approaches us with temerity and asks in the most deferential manner if we could possibly help financially so that he and the bass can get back to their homes. Neither band receives any payment whatsoever for this "engagement" and the only possibility is a rural bus, the fare for which is quite beyond their normal means. Of course we do, though it is quite difficult to get them to accept, and especially in the kind of pseudo-German by which we communicate through George, that we do it in gratitude "for the music". No, they say, the music is free, it is yours anyway because you heard it. The money is for us poor peasants.

But they make sure we are invited to the communal meal which inevitably follows. Meat-stew and bread. In such circumstances you take meat-stew with crossed fingers, but you take it.

"Nobody wants this music". They wanted it for the duration of the dance at Mociu, and fervently. But that does not sustain a livelihood, especially when the terms of the engagement do not include payment. Whatever servitude was commanded in former days there was always payment for services rendered. The cultural association responsible evidently has no disposable cash, since it relies on the nation, which is paralysed by corruption like most nations. And we distribute packets of coffee to the band's family, trying not to feel too much like Jehovah's Witnesses, and surrounded by their farewells fall exhausted into the car and drive off toward the next stop, Tîrgu Lăpuș, over the great bare Transylvanian peneplain, where cultivation is almost indistinguishable from wilderness.

The next news we have of the Soporul band, three years later from Popic in Maramureș, is that they were invited by one of the Romanian communities in the States for a festival, got there, and never came back. They got artists' residence permits and stayed on, indefinitely as far as we can understand. A silence grows in the green stony lanes of Soporul de Campie, in which no one tunes a violin any more.

"I am a Poet"

i.m. Barry MacSweeney

We were staying in Szárhegy, near Gheorgheni, in the house of a retired Hungarian couple who constantly fussed round us in the most charming manner, totally possessed by the instincts of "peasant hospitality" although they lived in a big village now only partly agrarian. He was a retired construction superintendent, waiting for a state pension which was already three years late in arriving. In their kitchen/living room we were given a splendid dinner with a delicious demi-sec rosé made by the man himself, and then went out to stroll the streets of the village.

The street they lived in: long, straight, unmetalled but evenly surfaced, other streets off it at right angles, a grid. The houses all one-storey, moderately substantial in the standard pattern, standing in their own kitchen-gardens with orchard trees and wells, wooden fencing round them. All individually decorated, many even with drain-pipe corners bearing flower-like constructs cut out of the metal – and equal: all more or less equal to each other.

We turned at the end of their street into a slightly more important road leading towards the centre. We passed on the right one of those long low buildings we've seen in many places, probably relics of communism, which people seem to have difficulty finding a use for. A row of rather high small windows in a dirty white wall along the street, doors at each end, and no signs of use in the windows. But the last window with its door, someone had been able to make into a bar: the white wall-paint newer and brighter for the last ten metres, lights on, a couple of tables with chairs on the sidewalk outside it, a few men sitting there. It had been a hot day and was still warm in the dimmed light of a pale cloudless sky.

As we passed by a man stood up from the tables, crossed the road and came up to us. He was small, about forty, with a drooping moustache, thick ear-length dark hair, and above all two big sorrowful eyes under bushy eyebrows. He took hold of my hand and continued to hold it gently, saying nothing at first, perhaps deciding which language to use. Then, still holding my hand sandwiched but without any pressure, he said in Romanian, "I am a poet. But my brain has been destroyed by alcohol." And his big mournful eyes gazed into mine while we nodded sympathetically and waited for whatever came next. He stayed thus a little longer, then without any further business he let go of my hand and returned to the bar across the road.

The Dawn Crows of Cluj

We were staying at the Hotel Melody, on the corner of the main square of Cluj. I woke up very early in the morning, went to the window, drew aside the curtain and looked out. The first yellowish light of a clear sky was in place over the square, turning pink towards the ground, and a migration of crows was in progress. They were everywhere, thousands of them, filling the air, sitting on everything in sight. There were long rows of them on all the roof ridges, they sat on the weather-vanes, they crowded round the spire of the Cathedral, perched on its protuberances and floated off again. They were on the statues, on the roofs of cars, on any raised point but never for long, and all the time a seething movement of flying crows between and above the buildings, in all directions but predominantly westwards, towards where I was. The queues on the roof ridges constantly changed, members floating off and being replaced by newcomers, moving up, sidling along, coming and going. A great stream of crows poured constantly above me, and the air was full of their calls, on all sides, far and near.

The architecture, especially at roof level, is still mostly "Habsburg baroque", with steeply pitched roofs, ornamental balustrades, turrets here and there. The crows wrote this scene deep into the past: sky and earth, town and land, Old Europe. Not just old but also Europe: British crows do not migrate. Migration demands a continent.

A sense of exaltation with a black heart to it, the river of crows streaming up over the hotel like someone raising a glass of wine at a funeral dinner, vast extents of land stretching away on all sides, plains mountains rivers forests, inhabited proudly and precariously, a great honour and a great dread, Royalty alone in the fields. The songs sung at dawn in small and scruffy main-road villages, as the first lorries set out for Vienna.

The Towns along the Tisa

O the towns along the Tisa, the flaking walls, the
ragged squares, Habsburg halls and communist
concrete eroding in the river wind... Border
towns stuck with closed borders, broken
bridges over the Tisa, holes in the roads,
buffalo carts ignoring the traffic lights... A
shepherd with staff and cloak stands outside
the Hotel Tisa, gypsies in orange skirts and
wide-brimmed black hats cluster on corners...
People wandering the streets hoping to pick up
some work or leaning against walls on market
day holding in front of their midriffs the one
object they've got for sale, a model house or a
packet of tea... The last offices in the western
world, heated by small wood stoves, desks
heaped with impractical directives, as the first
bits of snow descend and everything gets dark
together.

Kalotaszeg

Low hills carved into terraces, neglected now, full of wild grass. Shortage of young people to work the land, gone to building sites in the towns. Thin, gnarled, elderly men and women, digging potatoes in thin strips in the valley bottoms. They give the greeting, as always, and bilingually.

A dip rather than a valley, a long shallow trough with maize and potatoes growing in the bottom among fruit trees, and shepherds watching small herds on the shoulders. It is so threadbare and close to bleak that we have to remind ourselves that this really is Kalotaszeg, a name meaning to us a peculiarly rich and sophisticated music, with its immense dignity and regret, its air as of saddened royalty.

The young people went away, leaving their parents to work the fields. Became migrant workers, drivers of long-distance lorries, with the same patience, the same carved gateway into hope, gable-end elegance, a radiance of graceful gestures cut through necessity. When we reach the village (Magyarvalkó) all the gable ends, which face the street, are decorated with radiating semicircular structures under the eaves, with elegant urn- and bird-like figures pierced symmetrically through the wooden slats.

Cosmic ornament. The universe in attendance, round the corner, over the hill, out of sight. Signs of welcome on the gate post. And an abandoned collective farm with a row of big agricultural machines rotting in the sheds, completely unsuitable for use in this kind of terrain. And somewhere, the universe in attendance, geese sitting round the village pump, the woman striding up the hill twice daily to wind up the church clock, the old couples waiting for their children to return.

Like the sun and the snow, turning around each other.

Appendix 2006

I. THINGS CHANGE

The scaffolding is removed from the Endless Column. The "historic centres" of towns like Braşov and Sibiu are getting considerably smartened up for visitors, though as in most other poor countries the gleam and shine ends abruptly when you step into the living areas. In the countryside more cars appear on the roads, though the horse-drawn carts are still around, still with red tassels, now equipped with license plates and (supposedly) red lights at the back at night. New lorry routes are blazed through villages, covering everyone with dust from time to time (see *Sunday Evening in Botiza*) and confusing the street layout of lower Budeşti so that I can't locate the "oldest house" any more. Quite possibly it no longer exists. Half the "hotels" we stayed in no longer exist. Most of them seemed dubious institutions, staffed entirely by young women who appeared startled at encountering bona fide travellers. At Ocna Şugatag there is a gypsy encampment by the lake below the town, busy with metalwork over a fire. The spectre of enormous bureaucratic intervention hovers over the land.

Following again the walk from Glod to Poienile Izei in 2006, nobody notices us. No one stops work and asks where we've come from and where we're going. Foreigners are becoming commonplace. There's a scatter of *pensiuni* in Poienile. The hospitality remains manifest and sincere but more organised. The food is wonderful in daunting quantities ("Yes we always have mutton stew for breakfast") and you'll be shown plenty and told plenty but you won't be asked much. People with the right key in their pockets seem not to happen to turn up so readily just when they're needed. The Borşa ski complex has expanded enormously and looks like a small town scattered over the hillside. I don't know what goes on there. Unchi has died. When I ask about the "poor couple" in Hoteni I'm told that nothing has changed.

The woman who runs the water-mill at Hărnicești is as gloomy as ever and says it can't go on for much longer. The shop-café-bar at Desești has a half-built *terrasse* outside it (you no longer sit among sacks of nails) and a "museum" next door which like most of the small museums in villages is an undisguised shop selling hand-woven textiles. A man at a house just along the road from the parents' farm in Hoteni when asked about the pots festooning his house, including a tree (see *Goodbye for Another Year*) says they don't mean anything in particular, it's just the way we've always done it. Every time you ask you get a different story.

Romania joins "Europe" and is heavily suspected of providing illegal prison facilities for victims of the U.S.A.'s "War on Terror". The British tabloid press shows itself unaware of the distinction between Romanian and Rom and says we should all be inoculated against them. Mr Blair announces that Romanians and Bulgarians are both very welcome to Britain, as long as they stay away. Romanians declare that they have better places to go to. People in Transylvania, not all of whom want to go anywhere, express apprehension and occasionally hope. In Csávás a travel-guide from București shakes his head and says, "They can't go on like this. They'll have to collectivise." Collectivise? Again? In Maramureş they successfully resisted collectivisation under 50 years of communist rule, mainly by not answering letters. An old man who runs a small neighbourhood bar in Vişeu fears that he will be forced to close down because the veranda over the meadows where most of his customers sit to drink is built entirely of wood which he thinks is against EU regulations. The Romanian Embassy in London refuses to include *The Dance at Mociu* in its regular bulletin listing all new books on Romania in English.

2. THE MUSIC CHANGES

Further information acquired about Efta Botoca shows that he was a better-known musician in Romania in his day than

I had assumed, indeed there is a street named after him in Timişoara. He was born near there in 1925, moving to Bucureşti in the 1950s, and he died some time in the 1990s. So he was a professional musician from the Banat, who worked with all the leading ensembles and orchestras of the Communist period but his preferred set-up was a trio with kontra and bass, a "chamber music" version, which in that era of massification must have taken some determination. Otherwise he was a classic Communist era re-trained village musician.

In 2006 we encountered (in a *pensiune* in the middle of the wood-yard at Vişeu) a Romanian television channel which transmits nothing but "folk" or *muzică populară*. Rural fantasy scenarios. One after the other, by the hundred, singers with their troupes stand in front of the camera in full traditional dress, smiling sweetly, swaying slightly, with a backdrop usually of a pretty rural house front, delivering destroyed village music. Usually they have three or four young children in front of them, sweetly smiling and swaying, sometimes the children sing. Very little variation on this tableau. Sometimes an electric keyboard, guitar and bass in a hay-field. There was one older woman who sang a doină well, with mild ornamentation, in the same context. Nothing else ever happens on this channel. I don't know who it's for, the rural population itself, pretending that's where it lives, or the urban population remembering where they never came from. At the bottom of the screen is a strip, and if you telephone the company, you can, for a fee, put a message into this strip for someone who you know will be watching the programme. It didn't seem to be used much, but now and then a message would float past. Beryl translated one of them as, "Thank you for the cake, mother."

Nothing could be further from this than Efta Botoca, which is curious because he has, as I said, taken the village music and made it into something else and something milder just as all the TV rose-cottage Draculas have, even into something you could call "sweet". There is some essential difference. I think it is to do with retention of energy, or even passion, in a displaced theatre.

There is a persistence in the tone of attack which is moral. There is another musician like this, discovered by chance in 2006 by walking into a music shop in Vişeu and buying a CD because it looked vaguely likely to be interesting (the music shops, like the bars, seem to migrate monthly and usually share one proprietor or assistant with at least one other business in the town so that they're closed at least half the time). A singer and flautist from the Lapuş region called Grigore Leşe. He has an ethnic line in preserved music, solo, and as representative of Romanian "spiritual" authenticity, and he is also a professional bassoonist, but what he actually excels in is lyrical songs arranged with small band accompaniment, of an exquisite melancholy cast. A very strong, controlled voice, in the big-voiced northern tradition, beautifully inflected. Again a sweetness, a sad one, but out of the strongest and most energetic realisation of a fading culture.

Ioan Pop says every time he locates a good fiddler to work with, after a year or two he leaves for the USA – brilliant virtuoso musicians like Gheorghe Opriş and Dumitru Hîrb, gone to work on building sites. But the supply of rural fiddlers seems inexhaustible. In August 2006, in that same room in the wooden house in Hoteni, Popic showed us a video of his ad-hoc group, Iza, performing as on-stage music for a production of *Elektra*, a simplified and triumphalist Romanian version after Sophocles and Euripides, by the State Theatre Company of Oradea. With Popic were three violins including "Diavolul", with Geta and Voichiţa singing. Sombrely dressed in town hats and long dark coats, the group intervened here and there in pauses in the action or accompanied certain dumb-shows, but did exactly what it normally does: Maramureş music, songs and dances. The pieces were specially chosen but unchanged, still bearing their traditional texts intact. And the match was perfect; it seemed as if the music had been waiting for centuries for this realisation of its inhering depth. It wasn't just that the musicians rose to the occasion so admirably, it was mainly that the material they brought with them belonged there, in a Greek tragedy. Some items had had a "ritual" function (wedding and funeral) which may have helped, but it was the whole sphere of the music which was suddenly dramatic and even "tragic". And most of the songs were lively or lilting, but a kind of grim perseverance became evident in this context, within this liveliness, and on the track list is a song, musically quite animated, with lyrics beginning, "Let the fire burn you, bitter world!..." ("We always sing this one at parties").

No need to speculate on the obvious, concerning the long "peasant" histories trailing behind this music as they or similar trail behind Sophocles. Continuity itself is the only important factor, a route out of peasantry in both cases, or at least onto its border. Tragedies which I view as acts of lyrical expiation against Greece's development of a ruthlessly exploitative military society and the invention of urban misogyny (both honours shared with Imperial China of course). A music which asserts long-standing resistance to and subjection under, empires, nations and businesses.

And at the beginning of Sophocles' version Electra appears at dawn and sings lines such as "My bitter tears shall never end", and "My way is the way of the tearful bird" and "...I have no child, no lover / I carry my never-ending burden, / Washed in my tears" [translation by E.F. Watling]. These are familiar tropes in Transylvanian lamenting songs. Electra will never stop being sorrowful: she will either disappear when the act is done or continue to lament succeeding sorrows. She is masked, she wears the mask of anger and despair which she cannot take off, just as she can never marry, for her name means "the unwedded", another "peasant" disaster. Greek fatalism is heavy with guilt, but the chorus, the circular dance, the hora, brings a relentless music of unchanging burden up through Macedonia to Transylvania, or across central Asia with the Magyars, which resides insolubly in the most energetic dance or the sweetest love-song. The burden is worn not exactly lightly, but like a ceremonial robe.

But it also appeared that ventures such as this were at the beginning of a rethinking of the group Iza, which now tours round Romania and sometimes further afield as more-or-less a fixed trio of fiddle, zongora and drum doubling double-bass (Ioachim Faţ, Popic, Grigore Chira) with the two singers. Their normal repertoire for this seems to be reduced and fixed, though they have a mass of things up their sleeves and a whole concert of *colinde* (carols) can be seen on U-Tube. This is a success which they deserve, which replaces a long period of economic worry, but it is not what Popic's ambition was when we first met him – that was to "get the villagers singing and dancing again" with a fluid group of musicians drawn from among them. The end of social music seems to be irreversible.

Appendix 2008/10

THE LAST GYPSY THE LAST HORSE
THE LAST FIDDLER THE LAST EVERYTHING

Three days in Hoteni at the end of July 2008 after being in Transcarpathian Ukraine. An immediate realization that a great deal has changed rather suddenly. Coming over the Prislop Pass in a taxi in the middle of the night and getting down to Vişeu de Sus: a bright new supermarket, like an enormous glass cube, fully lit at night. Another one on the edge of Sighet.

On the second day we begin to notice things. Where are the animals? Why are there so few horse-drawn carts on the roads? Two years ago we counted 70 horses cows and buffalo passing the house twice a day on their ways to and from the open pastures. One afternoon two buffalo pass by on their way back to the village and that's it. We assume the pasturage has been transferred to elsewhere this season, as sometimes happens, but it hasn't. We ask and are told: the men are all working in Spain and Portugal, leaving the women and the elderly to manage the agriculture, and that's all they can manage; they can't manage animals as well, so they've got rid of them.

And the men come back with money, which needs to be spent, so the structures founded on communal self-sufficiency through barter must all change. Enormous increase in the number of bars. The market at Ocna is no longer dominated by beasts, but by furniture. The last traces of the old society will no doubt be finally stamped out when EU bureaucracy reaches these zones. Rumours are widespread, some of them are true. "You will no longer be able to kill your own pig." "Why on earth not?" "Because you might have dirty hands." "We shall not be able to make our own brandy any more..." "Why on earth not?" "Because we cannot be trusted." "We shall not be able to produce sheep's milk cheese for our own consumption any more." "But it is our staple source of protein." "You will have to buy your protein from the shop." Agricultural suburbia. Precisely the localised self-sufficiency which would survive better than any other structure in the event of large-scale economic collapse (as it did in Greece), is being rendered piecemeal illegal (as it was in Ireland). No more sheep-milking picnics in the hills. Welcome to the world as we have made it. "They can't take this away." They did.

But a lot of the rumours turn out not to be true, or if they are, agricultural bureaucracy realises there is a problem and enters exceptions into the code. And we can't entirely be trusted with our brandy either because, we're told, some people have been making it with sugar instead of fruit as a cash product. And it is the richness of a long tradition of social music which continues to supply the musicians and repertoire as well as the performance quality, of a group like Iza. And Geta insists, "Everyone continues much as they always have done," and she is the final authority.

Notes

Romanian pronunciation

Ş is pronounced "sh" and Ţ is pronounced "ts". A final I following either of these or N is virtually unpronounced, but its complete absence would disturb a Romanian. Â or Î and Ă are all in the region of the neutral vowel.

Only one or two place names appear in Hungarian, in which S is our "sh", SZ is "s", GY is "j" and the uninflected A is an open "o".

Terms & names occurring in more than one piece

Gypsy. I use this word instead of Rom because (a) it translates the locally used *ţigane, cigány* as Rom doesn't. (b) it isn't loaded with racial or nationalist implications. There is a class system among gypsies also, and gypsy musicians in Romania generally prefer not to be called Rom, which they regard as a demeaning term.

Maramureş: here refers to the "historical Maramureş", a small mountain-ringed enclave in the extreme north of Romania bordering Ukraine, where most of the rural depictions in this book take place, and not to the administrative county of Maramureş, which encompasses a much larger area.

Horincă: name in Maramureş of a locally produced clear brandy made from plums or apples, consumed constantly on all social and festive occasions, sometimes as an accompaniment to breakfast. High in alcohol – the commercial versions are officially 50% proof. Known generally in the country as *ţuică* or *zuică* and to Hungarians as *pálinka*.

Contra, kontra: an accompanying second violin or viola which plays harmonies. In the classic Transylvanian string band it is a three-stringed viola with a flattened bridge, which constantly plays three-note chords.

Saxons / Germans: A number of towns and villages in Transylvania were founded or dominated by the "Saxon" population. These were a people brought from somewhere in Germany in the Middle Ages by the Hungarian monarchy, and settled strategically, with privileges, to defend the Ottoman and Slav frontiers and to develop the region agriculturally. They tended to remain separate both socially and linguistically and flourished as merchants until they dominated the seven major cities. Under nationalist Communism they became one of the underprivileged minorities, encouraged to emigrate when they could afford to, or indeed sold one by one to Germany as part of Ceauşescu's drive to reduce the national debt. After the 1989 Revolution the great majority emigrated to Germany

Taragot, tarógató: wooden wind instrument with metal keys like a clarinet but with a conical bore, rather like a wooden soprano saxophone.

Zongora: a normal Spanish guitar but tuned to diatonic chords and with only five or four strings, strummed with a plectrum. The word is Hungarian for "piano".

ex-Party hotel: big hotels built during the communist period, usually of concrete, to house the hoards of Party officials who were constantly visiting towns all over Romania to supervise the implementation of various acts of social control, from tax collection to correction of local music and dance styles.

Notes for Particular Pieces

Arnota

The two spellings of the Romanian for "monastery" are, in order, the forms dating from before and after the spelling reform of 1993. Romania has the densest bear population in Europe, but they would not in fact ever get as far south as Arnota. In 1999, the year after this visit, the monastery was converted to a convent for nuns.

The Brancusi Monuments at Tîrgu Jiu

Brancusi. The S should be a Ş and the name be pronounced "Brancoosh" with a barely-sounded "i" at the end. In Paris Brancusi seems to have dropped the diacritic and probably permitted an Italian pronunciation.

The Road

The final paragraph was added in April 1999 when the piece was submitted (too late) for Rupert Loydell's anthology for Kosovo.

Unchi: pronounced "oonki". It is of course Romanian for "uncle". Mihai Tepei "Unchi" died in 2005.

The Funeral

For an account of death weddings see *The Wedding of the Dead* by Gail Kligman (1988).

After a lot of fruitless inquiries to medics as they came my way, I finally in 2008 discovered a reference in an article in *The Guardian* concerning superstitions about drinking water, which mentioned that if you expend a lot of energy and then drink a lot of liquid (not necessarily cold) it can happen that your kidneys cannot cope with this, and this can result in heart-failure.

Sunday Evening in the Land of Oaş

Oaş: pronounced "wash" to rhyme with "ash".

The best and almost the only audio documentation of Oaş music available is on two tracks of the CD *Roumanie: Musique pour Cordes de Transylvanie* (Chant du Monde 1992). There is a CD from Arion (France, 1997) of "Ensemble Ţară Oaşului" which is two semi-professional instrumentalists and a group of villagers got together for a tour in France, where they were recorded. This is effective, but a staged version. What you really need is the DVD accompanying the book *À-Tue-Tête: chant et violon au pays de Oach* by Jacques Bouët et al., Société Française d'Ethnomusicologie, 2002. There you have the fiddling, dancing and singing (– shouting) working together. It seems doubtful to me now (2010) that Oaş music survives at all as a social music, or possibly as any other kind.

Efta Botoca
The other musician mentioned, Mihai Covaci "Diavolul", can be heard on six tracks of the CD *Fiddle Music from Maramureş, volume one,* issued by Steel Carpet Records of Derby, 1998. I was honoured to have him playing for my 68th birthday at Hoteni in July 2008.

Over the Border
Secessionist: what is elsewhere termed art nouveau or *Jugendstil,* in the case of Oradea tending towards the Disneyesque. The name refers to the secession of Hungary from the Austro-Hungarian empire.

Small, strong, dark brown horses: Hutzuls (Romanian Huţul). To "folklorists" the red tassel is "to ward off the evil eye".

The Dance at Mociu
The "primas" (leader and violinist) of the band from Soporul de Cîmpie is Şandorică Ciurcui. They can be heard on two tracks of *Roumanie: Musique pour Cordes de Transylvanie* (mentioned above) led by Şandor Ciurcui, now retired. An entire CD of the band is issued by Buda (France) under the title *Roumanie: Quatuor à Cordes de Transylvanie,* recorded on a stage in France in 1992 and there are now several Romanian CDs. In June 2003 they were still in America but by 2010 Şandorică was back in Transylvania where he seems to work as leader of several different bands.

The leader of the Mociu band is Carol Tuli "Stîngaciu". A CD was issued by Lost Trails (USA) in 2001. See also *Transylvania, Erdély, Siebenbürgen: a musical diary* by Wim Bosmans, Brussels, Museum of Musical Instruments 2004 (booklet with CD). The band continues but when we last visited them did not seem to be getting much work. It has issued a home-made CD of itself.

hang the fiddle on the wall: Jehovah's Witnesses and similar groups have been recruiting heavily in Transylvania and similar zones for some time, with understandable success in conditions of deprivation. They are apparently fiercely opposed to the production or employment of music, and musicians who join have to stop playing.

"I am a Poet"

Szárhegy (in Romanian, Lăzarea): I use the Hungarian name because it is principally a Hungarian town. The Romanian name derives from the Hungarian aristocratic family which built its castle there. The long white buildings were something to do with collectivisation. I can't call the "sidewalk" a "pavement" because it is a raised wooden platform along the side of the street.

The Dawn Crows of Cluj

The city of Cluj is more properly known as Cluj Napoca, but I don't like to use the second word because it was added to the name by Ceaușescu as a deliberate racial insult to the Hungarian population, on the basis of a contentious interpretation of local prehistory.

Kalotaszeg is the Hungarian name for an area of west-central Transylvania for which the Romanians have no equivalent. It is still predominantly populated by Hungarian-speakers and has been for about a century a focus of Hungarian village culture,

CPSIA information can be obtained at www.ICGtesting.com
Printed in the USA
LVOW06s1111230315

431643LV00001B/55/P